How to Live
a Godly Life

The Biblical Doctrine of Sanctification

Michael Eaton

OM
publishing

Copyright © 1993 Michael Eaton
First published by Sovereign World,
PO Box 777, Tonbridge, Kent TN11 9XT

This edition published in 1998 by OM Publishing

04 03 02 01 00 99 98   7 6 5 4 3 2 1

OM Publishing is an imprint of Paternoster Publishing,
P.O. Box 300, Carlisle, Cumbria, CA3 0QS, U.K.
http://www.paternoster-publishing.com

British Library Cataloguing in Publication Data
A catalogue record for this book is available from the British Library.

ISBN 1 85078 315 2

Cover design by Forum Marketing, Newcastle upon Tyne
Typeset by CRB (Drayton) Typesetting Services, Norwich and
WestKey Ltd, Falmouth, Cornwall
Printed in Great Britain by Mackays of Chatham PLC, Kent

Contents

Foreword

Down through the ages men and women have battled with the demanding question, 'How do I live a holy life?' Some have argued that only total isolation from the world can accomplish it, but monasticism holds little attraction for most of us. How can we let our light shine before men while we are locked away? Jesus brought his righteousness into the rough and tumble of life. No-one could justly accuse him of sin, but he spent enough time with sinners to be called their friend.

Others have argued that a 'second blessing' of 'entire sanctification' solves our problems but sadly sin seems to leak in through the cracks while unreality starts oozing out. Like the early Wesleyans, we might have an amazing encounter with the Holy Spirit and fire, but one burning experience is not enough for a lifetime.

Some have 'majored on minors'. While purporting to emphasise holiness, they have actually concentrated on certain details of lifestyle that often reflect slavish commitment to mere cultural preferences rather than true godliness. Paul tells us that a religion comprised of 'don't handle, don't taste, don't touch' might appear wise but is of no value against fleshly indulgence (Colossians 2:21–23).

Exhausted from disappointment, others have come up with 'let go and let God', which sadly in turn produces passivity and ultimately disappointment and dismay. How many times do I 'just hand it all over to God'? What is meant to happen?

Michael Eaton presents us with an excellent biblical thorough and practical approach which covers motivation and means to pursue a godly life. I hope and pray that it will be widely read and embraced and that the biblical doctrine of sanctification will come out from the shadows and uncertainties of the current evangelical world.

God will be greatly glorified by a people who will believe and follow the teachings of this outstanding volume.

Terry Virgo
New Frontiers International

Preface

This book is a simple exposition of the biblical doctrine of sanctification. It is theology, written for ordinary people. It does not have many stories or even many illustrations. It is pure doctrine, written for those who want a straightforward statement of the biblical teaching about living a godly life.

A word of explanation is needed about quotations. I recommend the New International Version for new Christians, and often use it when I preach. But for myself I prefer to use the Hebrew and Greek Testaments, with various other translations at hand that I consult erratically when I feel the need of some help. So most quotations are my own translation. I sometimes translate in a way that brings out the point I want to make. For example some versions use the words 'consecrate' and 'sanctify' to translate the same Hebrew verb in the same verse. I prefer to use the same English word in translation to bring out the connection more clearly. On the other hand I personally know well the string of translations that go back to the Authorised Version as their fountain head, the Revised Version, the American Standard Version of 1901, the Revised Standard Version, the New American Standard Version. If my translations flow in the channel of these versions it is not surprising. My own translations tend to be literalistic and keep close to the word order of the original.

I am grateful to friends who have been a stimulus and encouragement to me: the people of Chrisco Fellowship,

Nairobi, Kenya, who first heard the substance of this book; the congregations of Vineyard Fellowship, Cape Town, for whom I expanded and rearranged it, and who first 'published' it as a booklet; Esther Awino whose questions prompted me to preach and write an extra chapter; Beata Kilonzo and Margaret Nderitu who read it as it was being written and for whom I changed a few paragraphs; my daughter Tina Gysling who did the final editing and who, with her husband Roger, travelled with me when it first 'went on tour' in southern Africa; Stephen Onyango and the young people who meet with me in Kawangware, Nairobi, most of them 'graduates' of the Kenya National Youth Service Christian Union, whose enthusiasm is a joy to me and who were yet another laboratory in which this material took shape. Such friendship and helpfulness is part of the holy life and is sweet and beautiful in my eyes. As always I am grateful to my wife who has shown special interest in this particular work and who encourages me to write simply. My thanks go also to Chris Mungeam who asked for the book in the first place.

Michael Eaton
Nairobi
March 1993

PART ONE

What, Why, When, Who

Chapter 1

Introduction: Seeking a Godly Life

Our concern in these pages is 'sanctification' or being 'made holy' or 'becoming a godly man or woman'.

There are two dangers in getting interested in the quest for holiness: self-righteousness and despair. If anyone thinks he is a holy person in himself, he is deceiving himself. One man who thought he was holy was the member of a leading religious denomination that we read about in Luke chapter 18:9–14. 'I thank you that I am not like other men,' he told God – or thought he was telling God but he was actually praying only to himself. 'I am not like other men – thieves, wicked people, adulterers, or even like this tax-collector. I fast twice during the week (what personal discipline!). I give a tenth of everything I acquire' (what sacrifice!).

But God was not very impressed with this holiness. The 'holy man' was just exalting himself, said Jesus, and 'everyone who exalts himself will be humbled.'

But if it is a delusion to fall into self-righteousness, it is just as bad to fall into the opposite mistake. No sensitive Christian can consider for long what it means to be a godly person without being tempted by the bleakest despair. When I was first putting down in writing my thoughts concerning holiness, it was one of the most difficult times of my life – although God has ways of making up for any trials we go through. And 'better is the outcome of a thing than its beginning' (Ecclesiastes 7:8). From the time I set myself to pray and think and write about holiness, not only did I go through terrible external events (myself in a car accident, my son hit by a car while crossing a road, an awful threatened law-suit), internal struggles (temptations to self-pity, bitterness, unbelief), ill-health in the family (typhoid, amoebic dysentery, repeated malaria), demonic attacks, misunderstandings by friends – but I was also gripped with the thought of how far I had to go in the godly life. What a vast distance there seemed to be between where I was and where I wanted to be. How vastly above me was the pattern of life that Jesus lived. Often I thought to myself 'I'll never be able to preach about holiness. I'd be too ashamed. Who can measure up to this?' Only the covering righteousness of Jesus kept me going. I was staggered again and again by the sheer grace of God. It takes a certain amount of 'despising the shame' (Hebrews 12:2) to preach about holiness at all! One is too conscious of how far one falls short of the very thing one is preaching about.

On one occasion when I was just about to preach some of the material found in these pages, I was feeling I should not preach about such things at all. I shared my feeling with a friend. 'Michael,' she said, 'remember that what you are currently preaching about is not what you are an expert in but what God is currently teaching you.' That helped me and I was ready to carry on.

These twin temptations of self-righteousness and despair that come to us mean that this subject of 'seeking to be holy' is a tricky one. As we shall see, our personal holiness is something that we have to be concerned about, yet we have to come at it indirectly. Holiness is not a subject we come at head-on. The godly life is important but it is a side-effect of something else. We have to be sure we know what it means that we are saved 'not out of good works' (Ephesians 2:9) but 'for the purpose of good works' or '*for* good works.' Sometimes the Scriptures pass over 'sanctification' at points where we might expect it to be mentioned. 'And those people he called he also justified,[1] and those people he justified he also glorified.' One might expect Paul to say

'And those people he justified, he also sanctified. And those people he sanctified he also glorified.'[2] But actually he passes over 'sanctification' and simply says 'And those people he justified He also glorified.' The fact is, Paul does not want us to bring in 'sanctification' when we are thinking about justification and glorification.

One purpose of our being in the kingdom of grace is that we might live a godly life. Grace trains us to live godly lives. But we must not think that it is our godliness that justifies us or that it is our godliness that glorifies us. Justification and glorification have to be things that are settled in our minds before we can think about sanctification. And even when we come to focus directly on the way in which God wants us to live, we had better not forget that at best we are 'mere servants' (Luke 17:10).

We want to think about the quest for godly living in a way that neither induces self-righteousness nor despair, and which is biblical in its mode of presentation. It is this that I want to attempt. In fuller detail we shall consider:

A. **What** is holiness?
B. **Why** should we be holy? What are the challenges and the encouragements?
C. **When** does sanctification take place?
D. **Who** does the sanctifying, God or the Christian? and especially:
E. **How** do we grow in holiness?

Endnotes

(1) 'Justification' is being 'declared righteous' in the court of God. It is God's reckoning that we are righteous as Jesus is in God's sight.

(2) 'Glorification' is what happens to us in heaven, when we lose all weakness and sin, and God's 'glory' (radiating holiness) is given to us. In some unimaginable way we shall be given new bodies that shine with the holiness of God.

Chapter 2

What is a Holy Life?

The first question we must ask is: what does it mean to be holy? What exactly are we looking for if we are gripped by the need to live a godly life? What is a godly person like?

In the New Testament 'sanctification' or 'holiness' means (i) the **position** of being saints that we get at conversion (1 Corinthians 1:2); (ii) the **working of God** in making us to be holy people (2 Thessalonians 2:13; Hebrews 13:12); (iii) the **habit** of holy living (Luke 1:75; 1 Peter 1:15).

Holiness is separation (2 Corinthians 6:17–7:1); it is ceasing to be babies (1 Corinthians 3:1–3), it is cleansing (2 Timothy 2:21), the opposite of uncleanness (Romans 6:19; Ephesians 5:26; Ezekiel 36:25). Positively: holiness is openness, Christlikeness, purity, joy, dedication, separation **for** God as well as separation **from** impurity (Leviticus 20:25, 26).

Holiness does not mean Pharisaism, niceness, morality. There is nothing wrong with niceness or morality, but there is such a thing as a good pagan, and the Christian's holiness is greater than anything the 'good pagan' knows.

Christian holiness is not legalism. It is not severity or harshness. It is not exclusiveness. It is more than morality. Non-Christians can be moral. Unconverted 'church-members' are often moral. The Pharisees were moral. Luke 18:10–11 describes a moral man. The Galatians were legalists, but they were not very holy. It is not 'holiness' to have a critical spirit. The Galatians, despite all of their high morality and concern for the law of Moses, were biting and devouring each other (Galatians 5:15).

Holiness is refusing defensiveness, envy, jealousy, vindictiveness, irritation, lust, self-centredness. It is freedom from doing one's righteousness to be seen by people, freedom from selfish ambition, from manipulativeness, from pride, from self-exaltation.

1. Positively **holiness is assurance of faith**. A holy person is one who is confident in God, sure of his salvation, confident in the word of God, confident in the power of the Holy Spirit. It might surprise some that I put this first. But surely it is first. Can one imagine God being pleased with anyone who does not trust him? God wants our trust in him, in his Son, in his Word, before he wants anything else.

2. Holiness is **fresh obedience every day**. It is daily openness to God, daily obedience to the Holy Spirit.

3. It is **graciousness towards ourselves and towards others**. We are meant to be gracious to ourselves. God treats us with grace. We are not to condemn ourselves when God does not condemn us. We might well know what it is to be ashamed of ourselves. But shame is not the same as guilt. Holiness is being gracious to ourselves and letting that graciousness overflow so that we are gracious to others.

4. Holiness is **endurance in trial**. It is continuing to believe God and his word no matter what God puts us through. It is trusting God for tomorrow. When we trust in Jesus we are trusting him for our eternal salvation. Yet we also have to trust him for our daily needs. Sometimes it is easier to trust God for eternity than it is to trust him for tomorrow morning. The Israelites in the days of Moses were saved by the blood of the lamb. But they then became pilgrims and had to trust God for their daily needs. Although they were heroes of faith in their being saved by the blood of the lamb and crossing the Red Sea (see Hebrews 11:29) yet they failed in not trusting God for their day-to-day trials and testings. As soon as they had some practical problem they would complain and moan. Very often they would be a hair's breadth away from God's answer at the very time they were

complaining. They would not go on believing; they would not trust God no matter what God put them through. Holiness is when you continue to trust God no matter what he puts you through.

5. Holiness is **consecration to God's work**. Jesus separated himself and consecrated himself to his call (John 17:17). He could be so engrossed in God's work that he forgot to be hungry and said 'My food is to do the will of Him who sent me' (John 4:34).

6. Holiness is **goodness without self-consciousness**. It is freedom from introspection. The Pharisee of Luke 18 was not a godly man. Amongst other things he was self-conscious of his supposed godliness. He praised God for himself!

7. Holiness is the **enjoyment of the liberty of the Holy Spirit**. It is the positive enjoyment of being led by the Spirit into the will of God. It is freedom from tradition, from ritual, from guilt, from condemnation. It is freedom for obedience, for the enjoyment of God, freedom to glorify God daily.

8. Holiness is **being open to the Spirit's conviction without losing assurance**. It is the work of the Spirit to convict of sin. But God has provided the remedy for sin even before he convicts of sin. Holiness is when we so trust God for his remedy for sin that we can be convicted of sin without losing assurance of salvation.

9. Holiness is **living in the sight of God**. Jesus told us that our praying (Matthew 6:5), our giving (Matthew 6:2) and our fasting (Matthew 6:16), must not be done before people in order that the people will praise us. Fasting concerns our discipline of ourselves; giving focuses upon our generosity towards other people; praying relates mainly to God. Whether it is relating to God, to others or to ourselves, our righteousness is living in the sight of God. We live for him alone. We guard our character; God guards our reputation.

10. Holiness is a **purity of heart that leads to a consciousness of God**. Jesus said 'Blessed are the pure in heart, for they shall see God' (Matthew 5:8). He was not referring simply to getting to heaven. The Bible is clear that we begin to see God in this life. Moses endured as 'seeing Him who is

invisible' (Hebrews 11:27). Isaiah was able to see God's glory throughout the earth (Isaiah 6:3). With purity of heart there comes a consciousness of God that is able to see his glory everywhere. 'Without holiness no person will see the Lord' (Hebrews 12:14). Holiness is an inward purity of heart that leads us to a consciousness of God.

11. Holiness is **living for God's glory**. This is one of the most searching aspects of holiness. It is when we have a love for God that would do anything for him. It is wanting to do his will in this world. It is living to bring about a recognition of God's glory. We do not get too upset if we do not get much glory. When people glorify us they are not generally glorifying God. Jesus said 'Let your light so shine before people that they see your good works and glorify your Father who is in heaven' (Matthew 5:16).

12. Holiness is **transparency, ease, fearlessness**. It is communicativeness. It is having nothing to hide, the opposite of being evasive. It is when one's conscience is clear with regard to God and with regard to man. It is being in the position that one is not afraid of anyone finding out more about what goes on in one's life. Admittedly, there are things in our live we ought not to share. Paul speaks of keeping one's freedom to oneself in certain respects (Romans 14:22). If one is a meat-eater one should not flaunt one's faith in this respect before vegetarians (to use Paul's example that most would agree with). It is probably not helpful to share too widely, points where we are vulnerable to temptation. But generally speaking we are to be open. It is a happy state to be in, not fearing to be caught out, not living with a guilty conscience, having nothing to hide. It is feeling able to do everything in the name of the Lord Jesus, giving thanks to God the Father by him (Colossians 3:17).

13. Holiness is **patience**. It is submitting to God's timing. God has made 'everything beautiful in its time' (Ecclesiastes 3:11). Our times are in his hands (Psalm 31:15). Holiness is allowing God to bless us in his time, in his way, without being panicky or in too much of a hurry. It is letting him vindicate us when he wants to, trusting in God to exalt us at his pleasure.

14. Holiness is **loving everyone everywhere**. Indeed the paragraphs above are simply a way of describing faith working by love. Holiness is loving people, loving God. It is loving with a love that is thoughtful, not merely emotional. For love is action more than it is emotion. God so **loved** that he **gave**. Love did something for us practically; it was not just a feeling. The Bible says that there is one supreme matter that we must focus on. 'Love your neighbour as yourself' (Galatians 5:14).

One might ask the question: why is it that Paul picks out loving our fellow human beings? When Jesus talked about the greatest command in the Mosaic law he referred to loving God and he called loving our neighbour the second command. Why then does Paul pick out loving our neighbour as the thing to concentrate on? The answer is surely that it is easy to fool oneself about loving God, but it is not too easy to fool oneself about loving people. One might think one is loving God; the real test is whether it leads to a love of people.

Paul says 'Do not be in debt to anyone, but you do have the obligation of loving the other person'. Then he said 'For the one who loves the other person has fulfilled the law,' and went on to explain what he meant. If you love someone you will not murder him, you will not steal from him, you will not commit adultery. If you focus on love you will fulfil everything that the Mosiac law was reaching towards. If you walk in the Spirit deliberately you will fulfil the Mosaic law accidentally. Not only will you fulfil the Mosaic law, you will actually go beyond the Mosaic law. You will start doing things the law never mentioned. You will love your enemies, you will pray for those who ill-treat you. Jesus put it very practically: Do to the other person what you would have that other person do to you. In other words, in any given situation reverse the positions. Imagine that that person is you and that you are him or her. How would you like to be treated? Think of it that way and the Holy Spirit will give you what to do. This is love – the essence of Christian godliness.

If this is what holiness is, it gives rise to a few further comments.

1. It shows us that we **need** the blood of Jesus every day of our lives. Who can measure up to this? Who can feel that a day goes by without his being guilty of sin? There will never be a day when we do not need the blood of Jesus. There will never be a day when we can say 'Well, today I did not sin. So today I do not need the blood of Jesus. I can look into God's face and feel good because I did not sin.' That day will never come. We need the blood of Jesus. The blood of Jesus is meant to be used. So do not try to live without needing it. Relax in the enjoyment of the fact that Jesus died for you. Feel accepted. When you fall from these high standards – as you will – get up and carry on!

2. We must remember that different people find different parts of the godly life, difficult. Some people wrestle with ambition, but others do not find this to be a problem. Some wrestle with irritation. Some wrestle with worldliness. Some with habits from the past. We are not all tempted in precisely the same way. Our weak points have a lot to do with our physical make-up, our temperament, our upbringing, our experiences. We should sympathise when others have weaknesses that we do not have. We will find that we have weaknesses that they do not have. If we understand this it will help us not to be critical of people who have problems we do not have. They may be tempted at points where you are not tempted. You may be tempted at points where they are not tempted.

3. If our description of Christian holiness is right then we require some powerful drive to get us to be like that. This is too high to simply leap into. God has to do a lot for us. We are allergic to this kind of living. Those who think they can take to this easily do not know themselves, and have some Pharisaism in them. We **need** God's Spirit. We need God's chastening. We need a miracle of sanctification to take place. But it is precisely that miracle that God is willing to perform in us.

Chapter 3

Why Should We Live Holy Lives?

This is not so easy a question as one might think. Indeed, if you have never asked the question 'But why do I need to be holy?' you have never seen the gospel of Jesus clearly. The Bible says we are saved without works. 'By grace you are saved' says Paul. Salvation is 'not of works, lest anyone should boast' (Ephesians 2:8–9). 'To the person who does not do anything,' he says in another place, 'but believes on God who justifies the ungodly, that person's faith is reckoned for righteousness' (Romans 4:5). Amazing! The person is ungodly, does not do anything, believes – and he or she is right with God! Paul actually says we are saved by doing nothing!

'But,' you say, 'if it is as easy as that do we need to be holy at all?' Exactly! If you are asking the question it may mean that the Spirit of God has shown you the gospel of Jesus. Godliness is **not** the way to 'get saved'. Godliness is **not** something we do to get to heaven. If that were so Jesus would not have had to die on the cross. Salvation is free! Heaven is free! 'So,' you ask, 'why do we need to be holy?' I give three answers in this chapter, and a fourth in the next.

1. Because any dealings with God must keep in mind that he is a holy God

'You are to be holy, because I am holy,' said God in his law given through Moses (Leviticus 11:44, 45; 19:2). The

Christian is not under the Mosaic law, but some verses from the law are picked out and are applied to the Christian. Leviticus 11:44 is one of them.

We want to have dealings with God. We want him to bless us, to hear our prayers. We want to live with him for ever in heaven. We want to have his approval, to have him honour us, vindicate us, provide for us, comfort us, guide us.

But what kind of God is he? When you are making a friend, or cultivating a friendship, you take into account the likes and dislikes of the one you are befriending. It is the same with God. If we want his closeness, his blessings, we must remember what he is like. God gives us salvation freely, but now we want to get close to him. But how can you get close to someone if that one disapproves of what you are and what you are doing? You are to be holy because God is holy.

But it is more than that. Because God is holy he is determined to get his people the same way. We often miss this. The reason why we miss it is because God is slow to judge. We jump to the conclusion that God is not very bothered about holiness because when we are careless God does not seem to do much about it. But this is to miss the point of God's slowness to judge. God wants **voluntary** obedience. Under the Mosaic law, there was immense pressure put on the Israelites to stay moral. Adultery was punishable by the death penalty. So was juvenile delinquency, idolatry and various other sins. Jesus was looking for something quite different when he said 'If anyone wishes to follow after me, let him deny himself and take up his cross and follow me' (Mark 8:34). Notice: 'if anyone **wishes**...'. He was asking what each disciple, one at a time, **wanted**. Jesus wants **willing** holiness. We shall be as holy as we want to be. God does not put pressure on us through fear of punishment in the way that the Mosaic law did. Rather God deals with us intimately and lovingly; he woos us with tenderness.

But having said that, it is necessary to say also that when

God does not get his way in his loving wooing of us, he is likely to do something more forceful. He is a holy God and is **determined** to get his people to be holy also. There is likely to be suffering for anyone who will not co-operate with the will of God. Jesus has bought us. He died for us. He did not simply die for our forgiveness; he died to possess us in every aspect of life.

God is light; in him there is no darkness at all. There is no small area in God where we can find a little bit of darkness. God will not generally hear our prayers when we want things that are foolish or sinful. (If he does hear such prayers, it is a judgement not a blessing.) He does not compromise with even the tiniest bit of sin.

2. Because everything God has already done for us is designed to bring us to holiness

Think of what God has done for us already. He has saved us by his grace. But 'grace has appeared ... training us to deny ungodliness and worldly desires, and training us to live sensible and righteous and godly lives in the present age' (Titus 2:11, 12). We who believe in Jesus know that we have been predestined, but predestined to what? 'He chose us in Christ before the foundation of the world *that we might be holy and blameless before him in love*' (Ephesians 1:4). We know that Jesus died for us, but what was the purpose of his death upon the cross? It was 'to redeem us from all iniquity and to purify for himself a people of his own who are zealous for good deeds' (Titus 2:14). The Holy Spirit has been given to us, but he is the **Holy** Spirit and one of his ministries is to lead us into holiness. When we read that 'those people who are led by the Spirit of God, *they* are the children of God' (Romans 8:14), Paul is actually talking about holiness. The previous verse is about mortifying the deeds of the body. To be 'led' is to be led into the pathways of godly living.

The fact is the salvation that God has given us is not an end in itself; it simply provides a platform and a base for us to become totally different people in many areas of our lives. The purpose of our being saved was that it enables holiness.

3. Because holiness affects our experience of the kingdom of God

Consider three passages of Scripture that deal with the 'kingdom of God': 1 Corinthians 6:9; Galatians 5:19–21; Ephesians 5:5.

'Don't you know,' asks Paul, 'that the unrighteous people will not inherit the kingdom of God?' He goes on to list some sins that make inheritance of the kingdom of God impossible. 'Don't be led astray. People who have immoral sexual relationships, idolaters, adulterers, male prostitutes, homosexual offenders, thieves, covetous people, drunkards, slanderers, swindlers – such people will not inherit the kingdom of God.' Galatians 5:19–21 has another list: 'immorality, impurity, licentiousness, idolatry, sorcery, strife, jealousy, anger, selfishness, dissensions, party spirit, envy, drunkenness, carousing and the like.' Paul adds 'Those who do such things will not inherit the kingdom of God.' Ephesians 5:5 is similar: 'No immoral or impure person, or one who is covetous (that is an idolater), has any inheritance in the kingdom of Christ and of God.'

What precisely do these warnings mean? Let us consider several possibilities.

(i) Do they mean that people who have **ever** fallen into such sins cannot get to heaven? Obviously not. The Corinthians themselves had committed them but were 'washed ... sanctified ... justified' (1 Corinthians 6:11).

(ii) Does it mean that if they had committed such sins once or twice, they would not get to heaven? Surely not. All manner of sins can be forgiven, according to the New Testament gospel.

(iii) Does it mean that if such sins are the regular habit of one's life, heaven is forfeited? One had better be careful before saying 'Yes' to this approach. There are some very 'ordinary' sins in these lists as well as some very shocking ones.

Think of some of these 'ordinary sins': covetousness, strife, jealousy, anger, selfishness, dissension, party spirit, envy. Some of these sins have been evident even in the lives of notable Christians. John Calvin admitted at the end of his life that all of his life he had given way to anger. He 'asked pardon' says his biographer, 'for his impatience and bad temper, which was part of his nature but of which he was ashamed.'[1] Did Calvin never get to heaven? The 18th century Calvinists and Arminians were endlessly denouncing each other and showed a great deal of 'strife' – one on Paul's list.[2] Did none of them get to heaven? Luther's bad language has been the embarrassment of his admirers since the day he died. How many Christians have life-long battles with jealousy – and do not do too well in getting victory over it?

What party spirit there is among some otherwise sincere Christians! Are none of these people going to get to heaven? For myself I cannot think that the passages in 1 Corinthians, Galatians and Ephesians should be interpreted along such lines.

Surely what Paul means is this. Any Christian who tolerates such sins in his life is **at that point** blocking up the inheriting of the kingdom of God in his life. God wants to 'give us his kingdom'. He wants us to know his presence, his power, the conscious enjoyment of his forgiveness. But any Christian who tolerates sin in his life – including quite 'small' sins or 'ordinary' sins – will find that he is blocking the flow of the kingdom of God in his life. Did Calvin forfeit heaven because of his anger? I doubt it. But I suspect that at that point in his life the blessings of God were not flowing very richly for him. Did the Calvinists and Arminians of the 18th century all go to hell? I don't think so – but their endless strife did not produce spiritual power while they were engaged in it. Those who do such things **will not inherit God's kingdom**, even though they be famous and notable Christians in other respects. At that point their sins block the flow of the Spirit of God. Anyone who wishes truly to experience the power of God's kingdom must face

23

this fact: without holiness there is no experiencing the kingdom.

Endnotes

(1) T.H.L. Parker, *John Calvin*, Lion, 1975, p. 181.
(2) See A.P.F. Sell, *The Great Divide*, Baker, 1983, ch. 3.

Chapter 4

Reward

We have considered three reasons for living a holy life, but there is a fourth. **We should live holy lives because holiness affects our reward both in this life and for ever**. The matter of 'inheriting' the kingdom deserves further thought.

There is a lot of teaching in the Bible about reward. Many are troubled by this. It sounds too commercial for them. But Jesus constantly urged us to live for the rewards of glory. We should not try to be more spiritual than Jesus! Jesus himself lived for reward. It was for the 'joy that was set before Him' that he endured the cross (Hebrews 12:2). Because he was obedient he is 'therefore,' that is to say **as a reward**, 'highly exalted and given the name that is above every name.' Another thing to remember is this: the reward is itself a spiritual matter. It is not money or mansions in glory or anything like that. It is honour coming from Jesus and is itself a spiritual blessing. One need not worry that the idea of reward is commercial.

Think of the biblical idea of 'inheritance'. Altogether references to 'inheritance' come about 650 times in the Old Testament. In the New Testament explicit reference to 'inheritance' – if for the sake of convenience we may confine ourselves to the explicit vocabulary – occurs in 48 verses.

Abraham lived for his inheritance. God said to Abraham (Genesis 15:7–8) 'I brought you out ... to give you this land ... to inherit it.' The land is a gift; its inheritance is future.

One might ask: what does its actual possession depend on? The mere passing of time? Death? A particular level of obedience? Abraham is already justified (Genesis 15:6).

In Genesis 22:17 after the oath of Genesis 22:16, Abraham is told that his seed will inherit the gate of his enemies (that is, the territory of his enemies, Canaan). The actual possession of the inheritance, still in the future, is **a reward for the obedience of Genesis 22**. One notes even at this stage: **inheritance is a reward for obedience**.

In the days of the Mosaic law, the inheritance is both **given** and **taken**. Leviticus 20:24 puts it clearly. 'You shall **take** their land, and I will **give** it to you to possess it.' This means that **there is a difference between the allocation of the inheritance and the possession of the inheritance**. One could have inheritance allocated, but not get it. It is this fact that gives rises to the double expressions that one finds in connection with inheritance. When one reads of 'possessing one's possessions' (Obadiah 17) or of 'the inheritance which you shall inherit' (Deuteronomy 19:14) one reason for the double expression is that it was possible for there to be a 'possession' which was not 'possessed'.

The Levites had no territorial inheritance. That is, no portion of the land was appointed for their exclusive use (Numbers 18:23; Deuteronomy 12:12). The institution of the Levites highlighted the point that the whole nation, whom they represented, were to be a people utterly dependent upon and totally surrendered to God. This was a permanent reminder built into the institutions of Israel that there could be inheritance directly from God himself without the **emphasis** being on territorial acquisition. For the Levites it was said 'the Levites have no share or inheritance ... Yahweh is their inheritance.' This means they would have the privilege of closeness to the presence of God in the tabernacle (Numbers 18:5–7). Their delight was to be in the service of God. When God says 'I am your share and your inheritance' (Numbers 18:20) it presumably means that God was promising to **directly** bless them, independently of the territorial acquisitions that others had. The institution of the Levites thus prepared the way for an 'inheritance' that was directly in the control of God himself rather than mediated through the legislative arrangements concerning Israelite territory.

Under the law, enjoyment of inheritance was related to legal obedience (Deuteronomy 4:1; 6:18). The Israelites were to keep the law and would lose their inheritance if they were disobedient (Deuteronomy 28:58, 63). There was however a possibility of getting it back if they could be renewed unto repentance (Deuteronomy 30). Although the southern part of the nation was exiled to Babylon because of idolatry, God kept their inheritance for them. When they repented of their breach of the covenant God brought them back.

There was a connection between the Israelites' having an inheritance and God's having an inheritance in Israel. In Deuteronomy 4:20 God is said to have his inheritance in his people. In the next verse the land is said to be the people's inheritance. The link between the two uses of the inheritance-idea is striking. If the people will be an inheritance for God's delight, he will give them their inheritance for their delight.

Why should we be holy? Because holiness is indispensable to our getting our inheritance of the enjoyment of God's presence, the enjoyment of honour coming from God.

Coming to the New Testament we discover that at **no point is 'inheritance' dependent merely on justification**. It is not received by 'faith only'. It is rather the reward for meekness (Matthew 5:5), suffering in the form of 'leaving everything' (Matthew 19:27–20:16), suffering with Christ (Romans 8:17), a personal sanctification which results from being built up by the word of grace (Acts 20:32). It is the result of **diligent** faith (Acts 26:18), and of serving the Lord from the heart (Colossians 3:23–24). It is attained by faith **and patience** (Hebrews 6:12), by a spiritual attitude to one's spouse (1 Peter 3:7), by overcoming sin (Revelation 21:7, 8).

There are both present and future phases to inheritance. It is the enjoyment of the kingdom of God in this life. 'Inheriting the promises' clearly refers in Hebrews to what is achieved in this life by diligent faith. Yet 'inheritance' also has a future aspect. One 'inherits the kingdom' on a judgement day (Matthew 25:34). Presumably Matthew 5:5 also refers mainly to something future. The new heavens and new earth is the fulfilment of the territorial promise to Abraham (Romans 4:13). There is a resurrection to be 'inherited' which is distinct from the resurrection to condemnation of John 5:29b and Daniel 12:2b. Mark 10:30 has the twofold aspect clearly marked: 'now in this time ... and in the world to come.'

There is also a connection between resurrection and reward. 1 Corinthians 15:50 links the themes of reward and resurrection for it speaks of 'inheriting' this resurrection. There is little point in verse 58 if resurrection-reward is automatic. How can resurrection motivate one's labours if every Christian gets it regardless of godliness or its absence? 1 Corinthians 15:41–42 means more than one thinks at first sight ('One star differs from another star in glory. So also is the resurrection...') and is meant to indicate variation in level of glory.

The difference between inheritance under the law and inheritance under grace, is that one required obedience to the Mosaic law but the other requires obedience to the Spirit. Territorial inheritance was attained in Israel by the law. It was largely external, material, physical, nationalistic, and could be attained by any Israelite, regenerate or unregenerate, who was externally obedient to the Mosaic law. There is an **analogous but contrasting** equivalent to this in the New Testament, where the starting-point of receiving inheritance is conversion but what is required is obedience to the Spirit. Romans 4:13, 14 deal with the starting-point (salvation by faith) not with how the inheritance is attained. Subsequently Paul will introduce an 'if' (Romans 8:17). The inheritance is not received automatically. A similar point is made in Galatians 3:18, 29 and 4:1, 7, 30, where (because of the particular controversy at Galatia) the subject matter is largely our standing before God. In a later section (5:12–6:18) where the theme is actual godliness, he warns that inheritance can be blocked (5:21).

The main point then is this: **inheritance is reward; it is this that is the central motivating theme in the New Testament**. Consider, for example, Matthew 19:29, which is part of a section that includes 19:23–20:16. Verses 27 and 29 reveal that the main point is reward. In answer to the question 'What ... shall we have?' Jesus speaks of inheritance. Verse 30 makes the point that there will be some surprises, and the following and **connected** parable continues to deal with reward (20:16 repeats 19:30). Its main point is not that all rewards are equal but that the priorities ('first ... last') are not what men regard as 'lawful' (20:15). Other gospel passages make the same point.

In the epistles, Colossians stands out as exceptionally clear in this regard. Colossians 1:12 and 3:24 treat inheritance as reward. The phrase 'recompense of inheritance' is what the grammarians call a genitive of definition and means 'recompense consisting of inheritance'. The Revised Standard Version and the Arndt-Gingrich Lexicon have 'recompense as a reward'. In Colossians 1:12 Paul uses the word 'qualify' or 'authorise' and refers to one's being put in a position where something is possible. The two verses together show that Paul thinks of reward as something that is open to the Christian, but is dependent on works of faith.

Admittedly, there are passages where 'inheritance' **could** refer to the final phase of salvation without reference to reward. References to 'inheritance' in Romans 4:13, 14; 8:17; Galatians 3:18, 29; 4:1, Titus 3:7 and in 1 Peter come in sections of the epistles where the writers are not dealing with reward so much as the Christian's basic position that enables him to stand before God 'justified' and so be in a position to live for God. In such places the reward-aspect does not receive heavy emphasis, although it is probably still present. If this were an exception (which I do not believe) it would not affect my main point. At least generally speaking, inheritance is reward.

Loss of inheritance is possible. This is suggested by Romans 8:17, but is more explicit in 1 Corinthians 6:9, 10 and elsewhere where Paul lists the sins that block the way to inheritance, here and hereafter, if the Christian is tolerant of them.

A difficult matter concerns the **Christian**'s experience of God's wrath in the final judgement. I personally hold to a high doctrine of the Christian's security of salvation. Yet the **temporary** 'fire' of 1 Corinthians 3:15 is a matter that needs further exploration. Or consider Ephesians 5:5. It comes in a section dealing with the outworking of faith, and warns that serious sins will be an impediment in the way of present-enjoyment and future-reward in the kingdom. (I think the double focus of 'inheritance' is likely to be found here.) It also warns that God's final wrath, although intended for the 'sons of disobedience', may nevertheless touch the disobedient Christian. There is little point in Paul's words otherwise. It is possible for the Christian to be – anomalously and grotesquely – a 'partaker' in wrath when he was intended to be a 'fellow-partaker' in inheritance (Ephesians 3:6 compared with 5:7).

Here then is one of the great motives for holiness. God holds out the possibility of 'inheriting' rich blessing. Those who sow to the Holy Spirit will reap something back from the Holy Spirit. They will experience the presence of God, they will enter into rest, they will know something of the powers of the kingdom of God. In some mysterious way everything they have done for Jesus will be laid up for them as treasure in heaven. None of these things are dependent on salvation alone or upon faith alone. They are the result of godliness, of sowing to the Spirit. They are blessings that can be gained or lost.

Chapter 5

When Are We Sanctified?

When does 'sanctification' take place in our lives? The answer is threefold. (i) There is a sanctification that takes place at conversion; (ii) a sanctification that takes effect experientially as we yield ourselves to what God has done for us; and (iii) there is a sanctification that proceeds and progresses all of our lives. We are considering mainly the 'sanctification' that goes on throughout our entire lives. But it would be good to get a grasp of the three aspects I have mentioned.

1. There is a 'sanctification' or 'consecration' that takes place at conversion. We are placed in the kingdom of God (Colossians 1:13). We are 'sanctified for ever' (Hebrews 2:11; 10:10, 14, 29; 13:12). We are 'saints' (Acts 26:18; 1 Corinthians 1.2, 1 Peter 1:2).

2. Yet something has to happen on the human side if this is to have a vital impact upon our lives. In Romans chapter 6:1–11, Paul tells us that we have 'died to sin'. We have left the kingdom of darkness and sin no longer rules over us. Instead the grace of God rules over our lives. Sin will not have dominion over us because grace exercises a lordship over our lives.

But then a few verses later Paul says something that may at first be puzzling. 'Do you not know,' he asks, 'that to the one that you present yourself to as slaves for obedience, you are the slaves to that one whom you obey? This is so whether it be slavery to sin (which leads to death) or slavery to obedience (which leads to righteous living).'

Now the second half of the chapter seems to be somewhat contradictory to the first half of the chapter. In the first half Paul said that we died to sin; sin cannot possibly rule over us; grace reigns over us. But in the second half he holds out the possibility that these Christians might after all be slaves to sin.

The explanation lies in the fact that there is a difference between our **position** in God's kingdom and our **experience**. My position is what has happened to me in Christ. My experience is the result of my yielding or not yielding to what God has done for me. We shall come back to this. My only point at present is this: sanctification is given at conversion but it becomes a living experience as we yield to God.

3. There is also a sanctification that takes place in the actual way we live. John 17:17, 1 Thessalonians 5:23; Ephesians 5:26 refer to this progressive sanctification. It should grow in all of our lives. 'This is the will of God – your sanctification' (1 Thessalonians 4:3). It has to be perfected (2 Corinthians 7:1). Love progressively 'abounds' (2 Thessalonians 1:3).

We already are 'saints'. But holiness is the enlargement of what we already have in Christ, working out in our actual lives (see Hebrews 10:10–19; Philippians 2:12, 13; James 1:18–21. We are sanctified in Christ (Hebrews 10:10) but we are 'being sanctified' (10:14) in experience.

The fact that we are 'holy in Christ' from the very beginning of our faith is a vital matter. If you know about the godly life but try to be holy without being born again you will end up worse than where you were when you began. **The joy of the Lord is the secret of holiness**. Holiness is not forcing ourselves to be moral. We must **delight** to do God's will (Psalm 40:8; Job 23:12; Psalm 19:7–10). We need to have our consciences set free by God's grace (Hebrews 9:14, 15).

God's method of holiness is first to tell us that he loves us and accepts us, blots out our sins, and sanctifies us 'in

Christ'. Then he asks us to show our gratitude and demonstrate in our lives that we have become new people (Hebrews 10:34; 2 Corinthians 4:16, 17).

Everyone before his conversion to Jesus has **two** main problems: guilt and defilement. We need clearing and cleansing, forgiveness and washing. Justification removes punishment; sanctification removes pollution.

We must get assurance of salvation before we start worrying about holiness. Think first about assurance, justification, forgiveness, sonship, your sanctification in Christ. These come first. Don't try to be holy until you have come to assurance of salvation. How do you come to assurance of salvation? **By knowing that Jesus is enough**.

> I need no other argument
> I need no other plea
> It is enough that Jesus died
> And that He died for me.

We must be rejoicing in our acceptance. We must **know** that we are accepted and are not condemned. The joy of the Lord is our strength. Holiness is **not** the way we get saved, but it is what we are saved **for** (Ephesians 2:8–10). '**Without** works ... **for** good works.'

Remember the differences between justification and sanctification.

In justification righteousness is **reckoned** ours.	In sanctification righteousness actually becomes ours.
Justification is a single act.	Sanctification is a continuing process.
In justification man contributes nothing. We do not justify ourselves.	In sanctification human participation is involved. We sanctify ourselves.

Justification is an act of God **for** us.	Sanctification is God working **in** us.
Justification is purely **legal**.	Sanctification is more than legal; it is God working powerfully in us.
Justification is immediately complete.	Sanctification is not finished until we die.
Justification removes punishment.	Sanctification is removal of pollution.

When do we become holy? When we are converted to Jesus. When we yield to God. And all our lives.

Chapter 6

Who Does the Sanctifying?

Is our growing in holiness something that is achieved by God or by the Christian himself? The answer is God does the sanctifying but the Christian co-operates in his sanctification. There are two sides to the matter.

First of all, we have the promise of God that he will sanctify us if we know Jesus as our Saviour. This is an inevitable part of our salvation. We are saved **from** our sins. We are not saved **in** our sins. Sanctification is **part** of our salvation. He saves us from our sins in **this** world. He washes us, renews us (Titus 3:5; Ezekiel 36:29). Religion is nothing; irreligion is nothing. Keeping the commands of God is everything (1 Corinthians 7:19).

The Father sanctifies us. It is part of his predestinating plan that he will get us to be 'conformed to the image of His Son' (Romans 8:29). This partly means that we shall follow the pattern of suffering followed by glory that Jesus followed (see Romans 8:17). But the 'image of His Son' begins to be produced in this life. We are even now being changed from one degree of glory into another into the image of Jesus. The Father has a purpose that we shall be like Jesus. He begins getting us to be like Jesus in this life. 'This is the will of God – your sanctification,' says Paul (1 Thessalonians 4:3), and he immediately goes on to talk about practical godliness in the lives of the Thessalonians.

Holiness teachers have often been fond of the phrase found in the Old Testament. 'The battle is the Lord's.' It was used by David as he marched out to deal with Goliath. The same thing was said by a lesser known prophet Jahaziel as the Israelites were going out to fight. 'Don't be afraid or dismayed because of this great multitude,' he said as they faced the united forces of the Moabites and Ammonites. 'The battle is not yours but God's' (2 Chronicles 20:15). This phrase has been much misused. One ought to note that these passages do not portray some kind of passivity. As David is shouting these words he is getting ready to do some fighting himself. When Jahaziel used these words he went on to say 'Tomorrow go down against them.' It was not a case of 'The battle is the Lord's; therefore you need do nothing.' It was not 'The battle is the Lord's; therefore let God deal with the matter.' Rather it is 'The battle is the Lord's ... so **you** go down against them.' Even though Jahaziel says 'You need not fight' (2 Chronicles 20:17) they nevertheless rise up early (20:20) and destroy their enemies (20:23). I do not know that these verses ought to be used in the teaching of holiness, although they have often been used that way. But even if they are used in the teaching of holiness it ought to be noticed that in the passages where these phrases are used, the believers are not passive. God is in control. He is promising to give victory. It is not that the people do nothing, but in and through everything they are doing, God is going to achieve his will. As Saul said to David: he is to be the one fighting the battles of the Lord (1 Samuel 25:28). They are the Lord's battles, but David has some fighting to do as well under God.

Sanctification comes from God. He is behind our growing in holiness. We do not need to be panicky. God will work in us and through us.

Equally Jesus, the Son of God, is the one who sanctifies his people. He is our Mediator. Every blessing comes through him (1 Timothy 2:5). He is made unto us sanctification (1 Corinthians 1:30). If we are given Jesus we are given everything else we need through Jesus (Romans 8:32). He is the captain of our salvation and leads us to glory (Hebrews 2:10). He is our heavenly Joshua. It is not that he is on our side in the battles of life, although that is true also. More important; we are on **his** side. He is the 'captain of the Lord's armies' (see Josuha 5:13, 14). We seek grace from Jesus especially, just as the Father is the fountain of love, and the Spirit the supreme giver of fellowship (2 Corinthians 13:14). The Father does not intercede for us; Jesus does (Hebrews 7:25). Our sanctification proceeds because we are united to Jesus Christ, as we shall see. We are intimately joined on to him and our holiness flows from him (see Romans 5:10, 21; 6:1–10).

Equally the Holy Spirit is the one who sanctifies us. He is the executive of the Godhead. He provides the new nature. We are temples of the Spirit (1 Corinthians 3:16–17; 6:19–20). We are sanctified as we walk in the Spirit (Galatians 5:16–17; Romans 7:6). He leads us in the paths of godliness (Romans 8:4–14).

But there is another side to this matter. It is true that we are brought into a holy life by the work of God, the Father, the Son and the Holy Spirit. But that is not the end of the story. The Bible also says repeatedly that we must sanctify ourselves!

The Bible never calls upon us to justify ourselves; it never calls upon us to generate new life within ourselves. It tells us that 'we must be born again' but it never says 'Give yourselves new birth'.[1] It tells us that we need to be justified before God, but it never says 'justify yourselves'. Yet when it comes to living a holy life, the presentation is quite different. We are urged: 'let us cleanse ourselves from every defilement of body and of spirit, perfecting holiness in the fear of God' (2 Corinthians 7:1). Philippians 2:12–13 puts it perfectly: 'Work out your own salvation ... because God is the one working in you. He is working both the willingness and the doing itself, and all for the sake of His gracious will.' Notice that Paul is not saying that we work for a salvation we do not yet have. He is writing to Christians. They already have salvation! But they are to work that out in practical godliness. The surrounding context is dealing with humility (2:1–11) and with being 'like stars

37

lighting up the sky' (2:15, GNB) in the way these Philippians live.

Yet it is not a call to total self-reliance. They are to get to a high level of godliness **because** 'God is the one working' in them. 'He is working both the willingness and the doing itself.'

In the Old Testament believers were called upon to sanctify themselves. Exodus 31:13 said 'I am the LORD who sanctifies you' (see also Leviticus 21:8; Ezekiel 20:12). But we also read of sanctification as being in the hands of God's people. Leviticus 11:44 says 'Sanctify yourselves, and be holy' (see also Numbers 11:18; Joshua 3:5; 7:13). In Leviticus 20:7–8 the two are put together: 'You shall sanctify yourselves and you shall be holy ... I am the LORD who sanctifies you.' Man's responsibility is mentioned before God's promises. In the Old Testament sometimes the 'sanctification' is purely a ritual matter. But it is not always so; Leviticus 20:8 mentions keeping God's laws. Certainly in the New Testament we are called upon to take part in our sanctification. 'Cleanse your hands you sinners,' writes James to the Jewish Christians of his day. 'Yes, **you** do it. Cleanse your hands! Deal with the outside of your life. But also deal with the inside of your life.' He goes on: 'Purify your hearts.' It is not merely the outside of the life that has to be dealt with (the hands); it is the inside also (the hearts). The point to notice is that James wants us to take part in our own sanctification.

In Philippians 4:13 Paul has been talking about handling money. It is in this context of a very practical aspect of godly living that he says 'I can do all things through Christ who strengthens me.' Notice he does not say 'Christ will do all things for me.' And he does not say 'I can do all things,' and stop there. He says 'I can do all things, through Christ who strengthens me.' **I** do it; my Saviour Jesus strengthens **me** and so **I** am able to do all things. The New Covenant promise is 'I will put my Spirit within **you** and cause **you** to walk in my statutes and you will be careful about obeying my decisions.' God works by his Spirit but the result is that

we take on the responsibility of obeying everything we know to be his will.

An interesting verse in this connection is Galatians 2:20. 'It is no longer I who lives,' says Paul, 'but Christ lives in me.' I can hear someone saying: 'Here is a verse that calls us to sheer passivity. We do not do anything. It is no longer I who live. Jesus lives the godly life in me.' But go on reading! Paul goes on to say 'And the life I – yes I myself! – now live in the flesh, I live by the faithfulness of the Son of God....' There seems to be a contradiction: 'It is no longer I who live ... The life I now live....' The truth of the matter is that there is a new 'I'! The person I once was has gone for ever. There is a new 'me'. But this new 'I' is alive. I am not passive. I am no longer the person I used to be, but I am alive in Jesus Christ and day by day I live on his faithfulness. Don't stop at 'It is no longer I that live.' Go on reading. Paul is not calling us to passivity. There is a new 'I' who is very much alive and takes on the responsibility of living upon the faithfulness of Jesus.

The whole New Testament continues along the same lines. The exhortations of the New Testament are addressed to the believer. Every command of Romans chapter 12 is laid upon the believer himself. These are things that **we** are called upon to do. We are strong in the Lord and **we** wrestle against spiritual opposition (Ephesians 6:10–13). We fight a fight of faith (2 Timothy 4:7). Who does the sanctifying? The answer is: God sanctifies us and we sanctify ourselves. We look to God for strength, for wonderful joyful liberating exuberant power. Then in the strength of the joy of the Lord, **we** cleanse ourselves from every defilement of body and of spirit.

Endnotes

(1) I know Ezekiel 18:31 could be quoted in this connection but that is a call to Israel who are already God's people; it is a call to a new attitude in the way they live (as the previous clause makes clear). The 'death' referred to (Ezekiel 18:32) is literal death in the fall of Jerusalem.

PART TWO

How – Basic Principles

Chapter 7

Theories of Holiness: A Survey

There are all sorts of theories about 'how to be holy'. Indeed one of the problems for anyone who turns to the books to find out how to be holy is that he discovers, if he reads widely enough, that there are a lot of competing theories. Most of the Christian books on the subject – including this one – are seeking to be biblical but they contradict themselves, so they cannot all be true. One thing that may help us in such a situation is to take a survey of different approaches and then take them out into the cold light of day and seek to ask which, if any, are close to Scripture.

1. There is **the idea that holiness does not matter very much**. I do not know that many people actually put it like that but there is the kind of teaching that goes like this. Jesus Christ clothes us in His righteousness. (That's right!) His holy character is reckoned as ours. (That is right as well!) There is no condemnation to those who are in Christ. (That's right!) Therefore God does not see any sin in his people. (No! That's wrong!) The trouble with this teaching is that it is too logical. It deduces from our righteousness in Christ that God cannot see sin is us. But no one who reads the Bible with his eyes open can believe such a thing. All over the Bible we find God taking notice of his people's sins and even getting angry with them. The truth is, it is possible to have a good relationship and a bad relationship with God at the same time! One's relationship with God may be good

in that one is saved and clothed with the righteousness of Christ. But this does not mean that God does not know about and take notice of our sins. He does!

2. There is **the idea that holiness is inevitable for every true believer**. This is perhaps the commonest approach to holiness today. It goes like this: True faith inevitably produces good works. If someone's so-called 'faith' does not produce good works he is not a Christian at all. The seventeenth century Puritans taught this very vigorously.

There is much truth in this approach. It is hard to see that anyone could be a true believer and his faith never have any impact upon his life at all. (This assumes that there is the time. I don't suppose the thief on the cross produced many good works before he went to heaven!) I know there is such a thing as an imitation-believer. A person who claims to be a Christian but is in fact pretending and has no faith at all. If you could get him to be honest he **knows** he has no faith. But the way in which this is often put is misleading. There are objections to putting things in this way.

(i) The New Testament gives separate and distinct attention to the matter of godly living. Ephesians 1–3 deals largely with our position in Christ. But Paul does not leave it there and assume that faith will automatically generate holiness. He evidently reckons that the godly life requires distinct attention. His message about the exceeding greatness of God's power **must** be applied. Paul does not reckon that it will take care of itself.

(ii) The New Testament realises that a true Christian may be grossly inconsistent. When a Christian fell into sin, the writers of the New Testament did **not** say 'Well, if you live like that you are not saved at all!' Rather they treated the Christians they were writing to as true Christians but they argued with them, rebuked them, showed them the illogicality of living the way they were.

If faith **automatically** produces godly living, we would not need to worry about it. We would simply concentrate on getting people saved and holiness would take care of itself. If 'A' irresistably produces 'B' one need not worry about

'B'. One focuses on 'A' and 'B' will follow! But the New Testament recognizes that a person may be truly Christian and yet one aspect of his life may be thoroughly 'carnal'.

3. There is **the theory that the 'baptism with the Spirit' is a gift of holiness which eradicates original sin**. But in my opinion this is not the right talk about the baptism with the Spirit. The baptism with the Spirit is more concerned with assurance of salvation, the feeling of God's joy, power for witness and service. It **encourages** holiness and it *gives a boost to holiness* but it is not **itself** being given holiness. The Corinthians were baptized with the Spirit and were full of the gifts of the Spirit but there was much sin in their lives (1 Corinthians). One can understand how this theory arises. People that have been powerfully 'baptized with the Spirit' feel as if they will never sin again. They **feel** as if they have been sanctified in a more radical way than they have ever known. But actually the power of the baptism with the Spirit is likely to decline. What has happened to them is only indirectly linked with holiness and certainly has not eradicated original sin.

Linked with this is **perfectionism**. The Bible tells us to be perfect, but it also says 'If we say we have no sin we deceive ourselves.' 'Perfection' is not sinlessness. There is no one that does not need daily cleansing, daily forgiveness. Is sinfulness totally 'eradicated?' No, the possibility of being inclined to that sin is still there. Original sin is not **totally** eradicated. Often a sin seems to disappear – but then it becomes a problem again. It has not been eradicated totally. Its power is lessened; it is overcome. But it is still possible to be tempted along these lines again.

4. There is the **teaching of the 19th century Keswick convention**. This is quite like the teaching already mentioned about the baptism with the Spirit, except that in Keswick teaching, sin is not 'eradicated' but 'counteracted'. The Keswick Convention taught **'Supression' and 'Counter-action'**. They said sin is not removed at all. It is simply 'counter-acted'. This is the opposite of 'eradication'. Actually the truth of the matter is somewhere in between

'eradication' and 'counter-action'. As we fellowship with Jesus 'we are being changed'. Yes, a real change is taking place. But it is 'from one degree of glory to another'. Real progress is being made but it is not total yet (see 2 Corinthians 3:18).

The old Keswick teachers often would say that we 'Let go and let God'. But this is too **passive**. In the New Testament holiness is a fight. We wrestle (Ephesians 6). We sanctify ourselves (Philippians 2:12–13; 2 Corinthians 7:1). It is true that we rest in God but this is not **passivity**. The New Testament teaching concerning holiness is very aggressive and active (see Hebrews 12:14; 1 Thessalonians 5:15; 1 Corinthians 14:1; 1 Timothy 6:11).

5. There is the **asceticism, or monasticism**. The monastic movement has taught withdrawal. Paul referred to something similar in his day (see Colossians 2:20–23). This is sincere. It seems to work at first. Certainly discipline is good. Occasional 'retreats' to seek God are helpful. But monasticism is not the way the New Testament presents the call to holiness. One always has to go back out to face the world.

6. There is **the approach of legalism**. The Galatians were becoming legalistic at the time Paul wrote the letter to the Galatians, but it did not lead them to holiness (as Galatians 5:15, 19–21, 26 makes clear). Holiness is not legalism. It is true that there are many **principles** of the Christian life. But Christian holiness is **more** than just following rules. We 'fulfil' the law of Moses by walking in the Spirit.

This list is not a complete one. One could mention also the teaching of certain holiness teachers like Watchman Nee and others. But this will suffice and set us on our way to asking the question: precisely how does the New Testament present the call to godly living?

Chapter 8

Union with Christ

We have seen in the previous chapter that there are several competing and rather contradictory ways of presenting the biblical teaching about holiness. This means that we want to be especially careful about keeping close to Scripture. It is important not to get one's doctrine of holiness by spiritualising some story in the gospels or in the Old Testament, or from a parable which is not connected with holiness. The places to look for one's doctrine of holiness are the main passages of the New Testament letters and the teaching of Jesus which deal with holiness. Although the whole Bible has things to say about the godly life, the central teaching is found in the Sermon on the Mount (Matthew chapters 5–7), sections of the New Testament letters, especially Romans 5–8, 12–15; Galatians 5–6, Ephesians 4–6; parts of Colossians, the letter to Titus, James and 1 Peter. We must go to these passages that deal with the way of holiness, before we illustrate the teaching from other stories in the Bible. This might seem rather obvious, but actually many holiness teachers use passages of Scripture that have little to do with holiness directly. I think of a holiness teacher who stresses 'brokenness'; his favourite passage is Matthew 26:7 where a woman had an alabaster jar of very expensive perfume which she poured over Jesus' head. A glance at the passage will show that it is not giving teaching about holiness in any direct way. It is a basic principle that when we want to find the Bible's teaching about any particular topic we begin by gathering the passages that deal with the subject.

So we now come to the heart of the doctrine of sanctification. If this were a piece of music the fanfare would be played at this point. When we look at the great expositions of holiness in Romans or Galatians or Ephesians, this is what we find. According to the New Testament, believers become holy people because they are united to Jesus Christ.

There are three main ways in which our union with Jesus is put to us in the New Testament.

1. **It is like a limb joined to a body**. The amazing thing about the human body is its deep unity. I sometimes like to put it like this. In Nairobi I live next door to a garage. There was once an occasion when I went out of my house in the morning and found that my car had a flat tyre. I undid the bolts of the wheel, took the wheel to the garage next door and said to one of the workers 'Please, will you repair this for me; I'll collect it in an hour or so.'

I also live quite close to Nairobi hospital. Now imagine that one day I wake up in the morning with a pain in my arm. What can I do? Can I do the same thing that I did with regard to the garage? Can I unscrew my arm, take it down the road to the hospital, give it to a doctor and say 'Repair this for me; I'll collect it in an hour or so?' No! I can do that with a wheel of a car but I cannot do it with a limb of the body. Why not? Because the body has a much deeper and tighter unity than that of a car. My limbs are not **screwed** on; they are **fused** on. They flow into each other. The blood-vessels and ligaments of the body cannot be broken without severe damage. It is a deep unity.

Now the believer is in a unity like that with Jesus. It is a deep unity, a unity of life. We are fused into Jesus Christ, 'grafted together' (Romans 6:5).

2. There is a second way in which the same point is put to us. It is **like the unity between husband and wife**. When a man and a woman get married something mysterious happens. They become 'one flesh'. It is very mysterious but

there takes place a deep fusing of the personalities. They become one in body, one in purpose. They affect each other. Offspring arise out of this deep 'one flesh' relationship.

The New Testament says we are 'one flesh' with Jesus. We are members of his body (Ephesians 5:30); even our bodies are 'members of Christ'; 'he who joins himself to the Lord is one spirit with Him' (1 Corinthians 6:17).

3. Then there is a third way of presenting this same point. This unity is **like the unity between a tree and a branch**. 'I am the vine,' says Jesus. 'You are the branches' (John 15:5). So the believer is intimately tied into Jesus Christ. As the trunk of a tree has life in it which flows into all the branches and so produces blossom and fruit, so it is with the believer and Jesus. We are in Christ. His life flows into us.

Now this unity between the believer and Jesus is a sheer **fact**. It is not necessarily something we feel. I might (but I never do!) wake up one morning and say to my wife 'I don't feel very married today.' She is likely to reply 'Well, you are united to me whether you feel like it or not.' Union with Jesus is a sheer, permanent, unvarying, unchangeable fact! At least two results immediately flow from this fact that every believer is 'in Christ'. We share Christ's position and we share his life. Because of this union with Jesus, according to the New Testament, we share in the main events of Jesus' life. What happened to him also happened to me 'in Christ'. I am 'in Christ'.

Think of some things that happened to Jesus.
(a) Jesus died.
(b) Jesus was buried.
(c) Jesus was quickened.
(d) Jesus has been raised.
(e) Jesus has ascended.
(f) Jesus is reigning now at the right hand of the Father.
(g) Jesus lives a new resurrection-life by the power of God.
And a future fact:

(h) Jesus is coming again to planet earth.

What might be new to many Christians and what many fail to grasp is that all of these things are also true of the Christian 'in Christ'.

(a) Has Jesus died? Then the believer has died in Christ.

(b) Was Jesus buried? Then I have been buried with Christ (Romans 6:4).

(c) Has Jesus been quickened? Then we have been 'made alive together with Christ' (Ephesians 2:5).

(d) Has Jesus been raised from the dead? Then we have been 'raised ... in Christ Jesus' (Ephesians 2:6), 'raised together with Christ' (Colossians 3:1).

(e) Has Jesus ascended? Then we too are ascended and have our home in heaven too (Philippians 3:20).

(f) Is Jesus seated at the right hand of the Father? Then we have been 'made to sit in the heavenly places in Christ Jesus' (Ephesians 2:6). We are where he is 'seated at the right hand of God' (Colossians 3:1).

(g) Does Jesus live a new resurrection-life by the power of God? Then my life is 'hid with Christ in God' (Colossians 3:3).

(h) And 'when the Christ, who is your life, appears, then you also will be made to appear in glory' (Colossians 3:4). We shall either be transformed and caught up with him if we are alive on planet earth at the time; or we shall if we have died, be immediately transformed and will be immediately raised so as to appear with him in glory. Either way we still will be united with Christ. What happens to him happens to us. His destiny is my destiny.

Now the New Testament doctrine of sanctification is the outworking of this idea of being united with Jesus. There are some great things we must grasp if we are to have confidence that we can grow in holiness. The first is the fact that we are united with him.

God has put us in Christ. The very second we believed in Jesus, God put us 'in Christ'. I cannot emphasize too much the tightness and the closeness of our position in Christ. We are so tightly bound up with Jesus.

What you need to know is this great thing that God has done for you in Christ.

You have died in Christ. Jesus came into this world and he came 'in relation to sin'. I do not mean that he ever sinned, but I mean that he was coming to take the position of sinners. He became a real man, taking our place in this world, coming as a substitute to live the life that we should live and to die the death we should die. It all culminated in the cross. Then he died. Romans says he 'died in relation to sin'. He dealt with it; he atoned for it; he dealt it a death blow. He left this world and never ever came back to the same position that he was in before. He was finished with this sinful realm.

But the Bible says that I am in Christ. I am fused to him, and I am joined on to him. What has happened to him has happened to me. If he has finished with sin, I have finished with sin because I am in Christ. If he has utterly dealt with sin, never to have to come back and deal with it again, then I have dealt with sin. I have finished with this world. In terms of my position I never have to deal with it again; I am in Christ. 'You have died to sin.'

Think of it in terms of kingdoms. Imagine two territories, two nations, two kingdoms. You were born in the one. The sin-kingdom ruled over you. You had citizenship in that country. Its authority ruled over you. But the day in your life comes when you cross over a line. You leave for ever that realm and you come into a new realm. You die in one realm but you come alive in another realm. The gospel is not just a little bit of forgiveness or a little bit of help from God. It is a transfer of kingdoms! You came out of the kingdom of darkness into the kingdom of God's dear son. You **died** altogether to that realm. Paul says 'Can we go on in sin? How can we? We have died to sin!'

Paul is not saying that you cannot sin; but he is saying that you do not belong to sin. The old person – the person you used to be – that person died. You are not what you ought to be, you are not what you hope to be, you are not what you will be – but you are not what you were! You have died! Even if you fall you do not go back over the wall to the old kingdom. Even if you fall you are falling in the kingdom of grace.

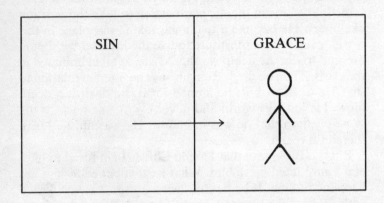

(Even if you fall you are falling in the kingdom of grace)

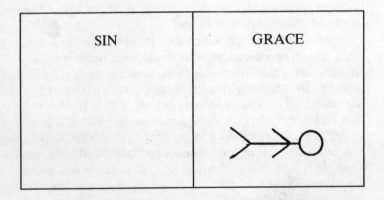

Paul does not say you will die to sin, or that you must die to sin, or that you are dying more and more to sin. He says you **have died**.

Indeed you have been buried, and you only bury someone when you are sure that they have died! That is what they did to Jesus. They wanted to make sure that he was dead. They stabbed him with that spear to make doubly sure he was dead. Then they had him buried. 'We are never going to see him again,' they said. 'He is dead and buried!' In a sense they were right. They never did see him in precisely the same form. That ministry had come to an end; Jesus was dead and buried.

But the same thing has happened to you 'in Christ'. Not only have you finished with sin, you have been buried with Christ. There is no way you can ever come back into that old situation. You have gone through a change that is eternal. You are never going to come back to where you were before.

So sin does **not** rule over you. You have been transferred into God's kingdom. You may 'feel' very much that sin rules over you but it does not! Defy your feelings! Sin does not rule over you!

Even when you do sin, sin is not ruling over you because you are not in sin's realm. You might fall but you fall within the kingdom of grace. That means you can get up again. You are not being condemned.

You might say: is this not dangerous? Might I not sin against grace if I believe this? Well, grace is dangerous! But God can deal with you is you sin against his grace, and he does not deal with you by throwing you back into the kingdom of darkness. You have died to sin.

This is true of you because it is true of Jesus. It is not so much that you have died; it is more that he had died and you are in him. If a prince of a country becomes a king, his wife becomes a queen. If a politician becomes a president, his wife becomes the nation's "First Lady". But in both cases it is not happening to her, it is happening to him. And it is happening to her only because it is happening to him.

So it is with Jesus. He has finished with sin. You are in Christ and it is a sheer fact that you have left the kingdom of God. You are a new person. Don't even try to live a godly life until you see you are in a new position.

Chapter 9

Risen with Christ

Not only have you died in Christ; you are risen with Christ. You are a new person; grace is ruling and reigning. It is powerful. Jesus was 'quickened' or 'enlivened'. Then he was raised; he was brought out of the tomb. So you – because you are united with Christ, are in the same position. You were dead in sins, says Paul to the Ephesians, 'but God ... jointly made us alive together with Christ.' When God made Jesus alive the same power raised the Christian. If Jesus has been raised, you have been raised. If resurrection-life was put within Jesus, resurrection-life was put within you. The same power was being exercised in both cases. We are 'made alive' by being united to Jesus.

So Jesus is in a new position with new power, and if you are a Christian you are in a new position with new power. Notice I did not say that you are able to **get** power; I said you already have it. In Ephesians 1:19–20 Paul prays that the Ephesians may recognise the power that they already have. God's resurrection power is already working in you. You don't have to get it; you have to see that you have already got it.

The greatest power that there is under God is the power of death. No one has ever yet been able to stop the power of death. Modern man with all of his cleverness can put a man on the moon but it cannot stop him from dying. One reason for that is that we deserve to die; we ought to die. This is why the Bible speaks of the chains of death. Death is the most powerful thing that there is, under God; the devil is the lord of it and he holds the whole world in fear of death. Ultimately all fears go back to being a fear of death. But when Jesus died that most powerful force in the world could not hold him, and the power of God broke apart that most powerful thing and took Jesus out of the tomb. It resisted the irresistible. And God did not just bring Jesus back to where he was. No, God made him the king of the universe. That was the most powerful event that there has ever been in the history of the universe. Jesus was made 'head over all things, for his body the church.'

But that same power is in you! You are in Christ! Do you talk about not being able to deal with sin? Paul prays that our eyes might be opened. God's power is there; but we need to see it. We are to 'reckon ourselves to have died to sin.' If Jesus has died, I have died. If Jesus is alive, I'm alive.

We read too that Jesus was taken to glory. He has ascended and is seated in the heavenly places. But this means that I am ascended to, because I am in Christ. So Ephesians 2 says we are seated in the heavenly places (Ephesians 2:6). Yes, seated! In the posture of kings. Our citizenship is in heaven – right now (Philippians 3:20). 'Those whom he justified, he glorified' (Romans 8:30). In connection with thise verse one might think that Paul made a slip and used the wrong tense. Surely, one might think, he should have said 'Those whom he justified, he **will** glorify.' But no. Paul did not get his tense wrong. In the mind of God the saved are already in glory. And if Jesus is living by the power of an indestructible life, then my life is hidden with Christ in God (Colossians 3:3). That is my position.

Consider this matter as we find it in the letter to the Romans. Did you realise that there are no commands in the first five and a half chapters of Romans? There are plenty of commands later on. Nearly every verse in chapter 12 is a command. But there are no commands in Romans 1:1–6:10. The first command of the letter comes in Romans 6:11, and even then it is not a command to do something but a command to know something. The significance of that is this. What is true about you is more important than what you do. Before you start trying to live a godly life you must know that certain things are true about you.

So we are told to 'reckon ourselves to have died to sin and to be alive unto God in Christ Jesus.' Now this matter of reckoning is not a terribly strenuous business. People get into an unnecessary heaviness over this matter. Don't turn this into a great struggle. It is the simplest thing in the world. As I write these words I put a little torch that I have at hand under my pillow (I am typing in bed!). I cannot see it any more. It is out of sight. But I 'reckon' it is there. I have good reason to believe it is there under the pillow. I put it there a few seconds ago. You would find it difficult to persuade me that it is not there. It is no great struggle on my part; I simply know it is there! Admittedly I cannot see it; I cannot feel it. But I do not have to keep checking whether it is there; I simply reckon it is!

Paul has already used two other words in Romans 6. He has said 'we know' (verse 6); he has said 'we believe' (verse 8). Now he uses the word 'reckon'. He says you know, you believe; now simply reckon that what you say you know and you believe is in fact true. The word 'reckon' does not mean 'pretend'. You are not 'pretending' that you have died to sin when in fact you have not. You are not pretending you are something which you are not. You are realising that you are what you are. Sin is not going to rule over you because you are in Christ.

If you want to live a godly life you begin right there by seeing what you are in Christ. Say to yourself what Paul said: 'I have been crucified with Christ.' Everything I used to be is gone. 'It is no longer I who live, but Christ who lives in me.' I have a new life; Christ is in me now. But then (seeming to contradict himself) he goes on 'The life I now live...!' But he has just said that 'It is no longer I who live.' How can he now speak of 'The life I now live.' The answer is: there is a new 'I'. The old 'I' has gone. I am a new person in Jesus altogether. I am no longer under the law. I have died to the law to live unto God directly. I am living day by day upon the faithfulness of my Saviour Jesus, the Son of God who loved me and gave himself for me. We have been legally released from sin. Our dying in Christ releases us from all of sin's claims (Romans 6:7).

But I must emphasize that all of this is a matter of sheer faith. You will not always feel this way. It is rather like what happened to Abraham according to Romans chapter 4. God came to Abraham and told Abraham that he would have a son. There was to be a 'seed' through whom the entire world would be blessed. But Sarah was barren. A year went by, then two years, then five years, and nothing happened. Eventually Abraham was old, over a hundred years old, and Sarah was ninety-five years old. Imagine having a wife of ninety-five and telling the world 'She's going to have a baby any moment now!' But the Bible tells us that Abraham 'against all hope' but 'in hope' believed! It was against all hope. It was against everything that was normal. It was against what seemed to be true of his body and his age and Sarah's body and her age. But God had said it so Abraham believed it. He faced the fact (Romans 4:19) that his body was virtually dead and that Sarah's womb was dead. But he also held on to what God had said. And in sheer faith – without sight, without evidence, without feeling – he believed that what God had said was true.

Now you have to do precisely this with regard to this matter of having died to sin. There will be times when everything shouts at you that it cannot possibly be true. There will be times when you do not feel risen with Christ in the least. There will be times when the devil whispers to you that you are in bondage. Don't listen to him. Be like Abraham. 'He did not waver concerning the promise of God, but was made strong by his faith and gave glory to God, being fully convinced that God had power to do what He had promised.' There may well be times when all the evidence says you are in bondage, but you must not be bowled over by feelings or by experiences. God has said you are alive in Christ. You must not stagger. You must give glory to God.

If you will believe in your position it will liberate you, because you know you are going to win. God has started a good work in you and he who has begun a good work in you will bring it to completion for the day of Christ Jesus (Philippians 1:6). Don't worry so much about what you are. Hold on to who you are (God's son or daughter) and where you are (in the kingdom of God's grace). Soon you will be rejoicing and this will give you strength and victory when the devil attacks you.

Sin has no claims on you. If you sin it is because you are listening to the devil's lies and deceit. The devil may be a roaring lion, but he is a **caged** roaring lion. There is nothing he can do. Walk in the paths of godliness; you will find he cannot stop you. Resist sin; you will find that you can do so if you come at it this way. Don't stagger at the promises of God. Go on believing. Refuse to feel condemned. See that you are risen with Christ and walk in newness of life.

Chapter 10

The Gift of the Spirit

Another aspect of our being 'risen with Christ' is the gift of the Holy Spirit.

There are conflicting views among Bible-believing Christians about the Holy Spirit. I personally believe that the gift of the Spirit is distinct from our first faith and repentance. I hold the view of the Spirit taught by the great Puritan Thomas Goodwin, and by the greatest English-speaking preacher of the twentieth century, Dr Martyn Lloyd-Jones. They taught – and I agree with them – that there is such a thing as the 'sealing' of the Spirit coming to the believer immediately after or maybe some time after his coming to salvation.

Perhaps you do not like that way of putting it. Well, I could put it another way. Maybe you would be happier if I said it like this: every Christian has the Holy Spirit but sometimes the full joy of the Holy Spirit does not seem to operate in every Christian as should be the case. Although every Christian has the Holy Spirit it seems that not all Christians are truly rejoicing in the Spirit as they ought.

At the moment, I am not concerned about which way you put it. Maybe you wish to say – as I do – that not every Christian has 'received'[1] the Spirit. Maybe you wish to say every Christian has received the Spirit but somehow the Spirit is not operating with the power that he ought to. Well, you and I are using the word 'received' in a different way, but for the moment we need not argue about who is right. Put it whichever way you wish.

But can you agree with this? In the New Testament Christians have power to witness, they are bold, they rejoice with joy unspeakable and full of glory, they have rivers of living water flowing from them, they worship God in the Spirit, they experience manifestations of the Father's love and of Jesus' love, the love of God is shed abroad in their hearts, they have the Spirit witnessing with their spirits that they are children of God, they have an instinctive inclination to cry out to God 'My Father, my Father', they have a foretaste of glory, the Spirit has been poured out on them.

Are you happy with that? More important, is it all true of you? Well, that is enough for me. Let us proceed from there. It does not matter to me very much how you get to **that** position as long as you get there.

In the New Testament holiness comes by 'walking in the Spirit' (Galatians 5:16). For Paul the works of the flesh are obvious (Galatians 5:19). He does not need any special help in the matter. Anyone who has the Holy Spirit simply knows that fornication, uncleanness, indecency, idolatry, witchcraft, quarrels, and so on, are sin. You do not need even the Bible at that point. The works of the flesh are plain! They have to be thoroughly cleared out of our lives before we can even begin to live a godly life. That is why Paul mentions them (Galatians 5:19–21) before he mentions the fruit of the Spirit (Galatians 5:22–23).

Then the believer deliberately follows the leading of the Spirit. The first item mentioned is love. It is mentioned first because it **is** first; everything else follows in its train. There is no joy, peace, and so on, without love being there first.

How then does this 'sanctification by the Spirit' work out in practice?

1. It begins by **consciously enjoying the Spirit's presence**. It is not something we 'take by faith'. We know we have the Spirit. One cannot be rejoicing with joy unspeakable and full of glory, and not know it. One cannot have power but not know it. One cannot have the Spirit witnessing to our spirit but not know it. What sort of witness would that be?

A silent witness? An unknown witness? A dumb witness? If you do not know the Spirit in this way, you **must**!

2. It is **when one is rejoicing in the Spirit in this way that one knows much about the leading of the Spirit**. It is worth noticing that the word 'led' in Romans 8:14 (and Galatians 5:18) is not a reference to guidance, although the guidance of the Spirit might be a part of the Spirit's leading. In the context of Romans 8 (and Galatians 5), Paul is dealing with holiness. He talks about mortifying the sinful deeds of the body.

3. **One aspect of living a godly life is to walk in the Spirit**. What then will this mean? It means following the promptings of the Spirit. One way of checking whether the prompting of the Spirit is real is to compare oneself with the New Testament description of what the Spirit is like. The Spirit is self-effacing. The Spirit is the Spirit of holiness. He does not glorify himself; he glorifies Jesus. Anyone led by the Spirit will reveal that it is this **Holy** Spirit who is leading him. He will be self-effacing; he will glorify Jesus. He will be led to be increasingly like Jesus, for the Spirit 'led' Jesus. The Spirit will prompt us to love.

To walk in the Spirit is a living and experiential matter. It means that one is conscious of the joy of the Spirit, the presence of the Spirit, the promptings of the Spirit. The Christian deliberately follows where the Spirit is leading. One walks in the Spirit, keeps in step with the Spirit, does not grieve the Spirit, is continually full of the Spirit – and so is led into the pattern of godliness.

In Galatians 5:16–22, after Paul tells us to 'walk in the Spirit', he goes on to explain what this will mean. 'For the flesh (NIV, 'sinful nature') produces desires against the Spirit, and the Spirit produces desires against the flesh. For these are contrary to each other, to prevent you from doing the things that you want.'

There are three items mentioned here: the Holy Spirit, the flesh and you. When a person becomes a Christian he immediately has the Holy Spirit. From that point on he experiences a battle within himself. He has the Holy Spirit but he also has a remaining sinful nature. His conversion did not get rid of his sinful nature altogether. The Holy Spirit is pulling one way; the flesh is pulling another way. 'You' are somewhere in the middle! You are conscious of the Holy Spirit; you are conscious of the flesh. You will have impulses to pride, to greed, to impurity. You also have longings to obey the Lord, to please him. You are so grateful that he has saved and forgiven you and cleansed your conscience. Sometimes you feel you will never sin again, but then you know that there are these impulses that come from the flesh and you know about them as well. The flesh seems to stop you from being perfectly holy. The Spirit seems to stop you from being perfectly sinful. They are opposed to each other attempting to stop **you** from doing what you want either way, in the direction of sin or in the direction of godliness.

Which one of these powers is going to win? The answer is: the one that you yield to. If you yield to the flesh, the flesh will get the upper hand and the Spirit will be grieved. If you yield to the Spirit he will have liberty in your life, and the flesh will be restrained. But neither the Holy Spirit nor the flesh give up easily. Even when one is enjoying a happy relationship with God the flesh has ways of sneaking in and catching us on our blind side. Often there will be times when we let the flesh get in and have to go back to the Lord and say 'Father I'm sorry!', and be cleansed by the blood of Jesus.

And so we go on walking in the Holy Spirit: listening to the Spirit's voice in the Scriptures and sometimes (as in Acts 8:29) even distinct from the Scriptures, pursuing the pathway of love in every situation, using our minds with the love of the Spirit, following every impulse to pray that the Spirit gives us, mortifying the wicked impulses that arise from our fallen bodies (Romans 8:13), enjoying the love of God shed abroad in our hearts by the Spirit. Then we will be 'led' by the Spirit into God's will for our lives. There will be avenues of service to follow. We shall find that we have gifts that the Spirit has given us, many of them quite ordinary, some of them perhaps more dramatic. Having gifts that differ we use them, depending on the Spirit as we do so.

Endnote

(1) I know every Christian 'has' the Spirit (Romans 8:9), but a study of the word 'received' in the New Testament references to the Spirit will reveal that it is referring to something conscious and experiential.

Chapter 11

Yielding to God

I said in an earlier chapter that there are phases in our holiness. In a sense we get holiness instantly at conversion. We immediately become saints; we immediately die to sin. But I said also that there is a second phase in our becoming holy. The holiness that we have in Christ does not really achieve much for us practically until we yield ourselves to God. Romans 6:16 says 'Don't you know that to whatever you present yourselves to as slaves for obedience – you are indeed slaves of that one you obey, whether it be sin (which leads to death) or obedience (which leads to righteousness).' Sanctification gets moving when we give ourselves to the Lord.

The wonderful things that Paul says in Romans 6:1–14 are followed by Romans 6:15–23. You can be thrilled and moved by Romans 6:1–14 but it will not do you any good until you take seriously Romans 6:15–23. You could agree with everything I have written so far yet it might not help you in the least. Romans 6:1–14 is followed by Romans 6:15–23. Having said most moving things about having died to sin he then surprises us in verse 16. Now this seems like a contradiction. You might say 'Paul you just told me that I have died to sin, that my old man is gone, that sin will never rule and reign over me. But now you tell me that I might become a slave of sin after all!' The answer is: being raised in Christ is not enough. The fact that we have been raised in Christ does not automatically mean that you are going to live a godly life. If it were automatic Paul would not have needed to write Romans 6:15–23. It is one thing to have a position in Christ but it will not actually do anything for you until you totally and utterly give yourself away to Jesus. The fact that you have become risen in Christ requires and makes it possible that you now give yourself to the Lord. This holiness that you have been given in Christ will not work in experience until you do so.

Paul wants to make this very practical. His way of making it practical is to tell us that we have to do it a bit at a time. You give yourself as a living sacrifice. You give your members. What are the members? They are all the bits and pieces of your life. The reason we have to put it this way is that we deceive ourselves unless we give ourselves to God piece by piece. We might say 'I give you my life' but we do not realise that we are holding back a bit. So you give God the 'members of your body'. You give him your body, your eyes, your hands, your brain, your feet, your health, your intellect. You give your mind to him.

You may know Frances Havergal's great hymn. She begins:

> Take my life, and let it be
> Consecrated, Lord, to thee.

Then she begins to break it down into its bits and pieces:

> Take my moments and my days
> Let them flow in ceaseless praise.
>
> Take my hands, and let them move
> At the impulse of Thy love;
> Take my feet, and let them be
> Swift and beautiful for Thee.

This is what it means to yield our members. On she goes:

68

Take my voice, and let me sing
Always, only, for my King;
Take my lips, and let them be
Filled with messages from Thee.

Then she comes to something not part of her 'body' in a narrow sense but part of the circumstances she is in:

Take my silver and my gold,
Not a mite would I withhold;

Then back to the different aspects of her life:

Take my intellect, and use
Every power as Thou shalt choose.

Take my will, and make it Thine;
It shall be no longer mine;
Take my heart, it is Thine own;
It shall be Thy royal throne.

Take my love; my Lord, I pour
At Thy feet its treasure store;
Take myself, and I will be
Ever, only, all, for thee.

This is the way to give ourselves to God. It will not be a practical matter unless we do it a bit at a time. It can be a great battle. Sometimes we are very conscious of areas in which we are defensive and self-protective. You may have a struggle to get there. Many others have had a great battle before you. If the only thing you can say is 'Lord, I am willing to be made willing...', then start there! Then give him everything. You say 'Lord, I give you my feet. I am not going to walk anywhere you would disapprove of. I am going to go to places where you want me to go.' Think of it positively ('I'll go where you send me') more than negatively ('I'll not go where you forbid me'), although both are involved. Say: 'Lord, I am giving you my eyes. I'm going to look at things you would be happy with me looking at. I give you my tongue' – the hardest thing of all. You say 'You can have my home, my salary.' You give the bits and pieces of your life.

You give also the bad bits. You give your shame to the Lord. There is perhaps something you have done that you feel so bad about. Give it to God. You give him your successes; you give him your failures. You give your emotions, your background. Perhaps you have had a rough upbringing, perhaps you feel unloved, maybe you feel you have no friends. Even in the midst of a crowd you feel so lonely. Give it all to God. All the bits and pieces of your life. You give him your future, your habits, your husband or wife, your career.

If you, as one who is already alive from the dead, as one seated in the heavenly places, already having a life hidden with Christ in God – if you will yield to what God has done for you and hand yourself over, I promise you, you will find that the process of sanctification is working in your life. You will begin to live for God. You will have a liberty, freedom, power. But I must warn you that Romans 6:1–14 won't work without Romans 6:15–23. It is not enough to have a position. You can have a position of freedom but an experience of bondage. You can be alive in Christ but because you are yielding to something you should not yield to, you fall into an experience of bondage. A Christian can be in bondage in experience even though he is liberated in his position. Because he is not giving himself over as one who is alive to God, he is getting into bondage and bad habits. If you begin to obey sin you will be setting up a mastery. Slavery is coming in again – even though you are risen in Christ.

So this resurrection power will not flow until you give yourself clean away. Have you ever done that? If you hold on to your life, you lose it. But he who loses his life for Jesus' sake will find it. Have you ever lost your life? Just give it away utterly, forget it. There will be some parts you are scared of. Then just tell him. Say to him 'Lord I am frightened of doing this. But I am doing it anyway.' Even that friendship. Even that corrupt source of money that you feel you need so much. Tell the Lord you recognize that he owns you. He has bought you. Every little bit of your life and experience has been bought by the blood of Jesus.

If you give yourself clean away to God you will make three discoveries, according to Romans 12:1–2.

1. You will discover that the will of God for you is good. You maybe thought that his will might be painful for you. But you will discover that he does not put you in a place you don't fit. His plan for you will be perfectly designed. Happiness is being in the will of God. The will of God fits the way you are made.

2. You will discover that the will of God is acceptable. You were fearful that God would ask something of you that you could not accept.

3. You will discover that the will of God is perfect. It actually surpasses your wildest dreams. Had you been given everything you thought you wanted it would not have been better than what God gives you when you give yourself to him.

Why should you not give yourself to God right now? If you have believed in Jesus you already have the resurrection power of Jesus flowing through you, but now hand your life totally utterly to God. Do it a bit at a time. Resurrection power will flow in your life. You will be 'led' by the Spirit into the pathways of righteousness. You will become a man or a woman of love, of graciousness, of peace, of joy.

Chapter 12

Fellowship with Jesus

We have seen that the root of our sanctification is to be found in our having died to sin and in our having been raised to new life in Jesus. This does not work automatically however; we are told that we must also **yield** ourselves to God as those who have been raised from the dead. It is this that enables us to walk in newness of life.

The next thing that the New Testament emphasizes is that holiness is a matter of walking in fellowship with Jesus day by day. We are not sanctified by a law or a system. We are not sanctified by a programme or a discipline or a theology – not even the theology of sanctification. We are sanctified by a person: Jesus. We have to learn to eat of him and drink of him. Unless we eat of him and drink of him we shall have no life – no liveliness – in us.

John chapter 6 is perhaps the classic place of Scripture where this matter is put to us. The chapter begins (6:1–15) by Jesus working a wonderful miracle: the creation of an abundant provision of food for a 'great multitude' (6:5). Such abundant provision is given them that there is plenty left over; twelve baskets of it (6:12–13). After the story of the walking on the water (6:16–21), Jesus comes back to the matter of the miracle of provision and applies it to the people. The multitude gather again (6:22–25). Jesus tells them not to be so bothered about material blessings. They

like the idea of someone who will provide daily bread but
Jesus tells them not to worry so much about loaves of bread
(6:26–27); they must labour for a different kind of food
altogether (6:27). They ask for more information (6:28)
and Jesus tells them that this 'labouring' is labouring to
believe (6:29). Still having the provision of literal food in
mind, they recall how food simply fell from heaven in the
days of Moses (6:30–31).

Now Jesus comes to his main point: He is the food, the
'manna' or 'bread' from heaven.

1. **Jesus is to be our daily food.** We are in a living personal relationship to him. Many of us, when we get up in
the morning, start the day with some kind of food. Even
among the poorest people, the day might be started with
some kind of bread and drink. It is one of the first things to
be done, after arising in the morning. We get some kind of
food to keep us going during the day. It may be minutes
after we have risen from sleep; it might be after an hour or
so. But all over the world, most people start the day with
some kind of bread and some kind of drink to keep them
going during that day.

So it is in the Christian life. So it is with the life of
godliness. The secret of growth, of liveliness, of strength, is
to feed on Jesus himself.

I emphasize that it is Jesus **himself** who is our food. It is
not exactly saying that the **Bible** is our daily food. You ask:
'But surely we meet Jesus in the pages of the Bible. There is
no difference between reading our Bibles and meeting with
Jesus.' There is a difference! The Pharisees who crucified
Jesus were thoroughly familiar with their Bibles – the Old
Testament. Jesus said to them 'You search the Scriptures
because you think that it is in **them** that you will find eternal
life, but you will not come to me that you might have life.'
They read their Bibles but they would not come to Jesus!
There is a difference.

Of course I am not criticising the Bible. I personally
spend hours with my Bible in Greek and Hebrew, every
day. But there is a difference between being Bible-taught

and Spirit-taught (as A.W. Tozer used to put it). This matter of feeding on Jesus is not simply a matter of reading the Bible and saying a few prayers. It is a matter of deliberately seeking personal friendship and conversation with a person, Jesus himself. For some people (I am one of them) it may be necessary to deliberately hold back from reading the Bible for a while in order to deliberately concentrate on Jesus himself. Then when one comes to the reading of the Word of God one is **already** in conversation and fellowship with Jesus and one continues the conversation with Jesus, as you go to his Word. **Two** of you are going to the Word of God together and Jesus will do for you what he did for the disciples on the road to Emmaus. He will point out to you in the Scriptures the things concerning himself.

2. **Getting this food requires some labour**. Jesus talks about 'labouring' (6:27). It is deliberately cultivating the fellowship of Jesus day by day. In the story of the Israelites in the wilderness they had to go out almost every day (except the Sabbath) and collect the manna. They could not generally collect two days' supplies. It was – leaving aside the matter of the Sabbath – a daily matter. So it is with the Christian. He must daily make sure that he gets some 'manna', some enjoyment of the presence of Jesus. He does so by faith. It is not **initially** a matter of cultivating any kind of feeling, although feelings of joy will of course arise as you fellowship with Jesus. But the feeling in itself is not very important. You might have a feeling of excitement if you go to meet a president or cabinet minister. But you don't concentrate on the excitement. You concentrate on the person you are meeting and what he thinks about you and what he will say to you. So it is when meeting Jesus every day.

3. **The result of this daily feeding is 'life'**. I do not believe Jesus is talking here about 'getting saved' in the traditional sense of that phrase. He is referring to the actual experience of being made alert and lively and energetic by the presence of Jesus himself in our lives. A person who lives

this way finds that he never gets hungry (6:35) and never gets thirsty (6:35).

As the story goes on the Jews find all this talk a bit hard to take (6:41–42). Jesus goes on to explain a little further. This daily feeding on Jesus is the same as being taught by God himself (6:45); it involves daily 'coming' to Jesus (6:45). It gives life and delivers from death (6:47–50). It is feeding on Jesus himself. Jesus himself is full of life; he is 'living' bread (6:51).

As Jesus comes to the end of his urging them to feed on him he brings in something he had not mentioned earlier. The particular aspects of Jesus that they are to feed on are his death (mentioned for the first time in verse 51). Jesus gives them a hint of what he is going to do: He will literally give himself to die on the cross. They are to feed on Jesus as the one who dies for them. In their deliberately cultivating a fellowship with Jesus it is the fact that this One has done something decisive on the cross that they remember. From this point on this very matter is developed by Jesus. They must eat his flesh; they must drink his blood (6:56). In verse 56 we come to a crucial matter: it is precisely this that is **abiding** in Christ. It is precisely by this feeding on Jesus that Jesus **abides** in them. He stays in them, putting forward into their lives his own energy and spiritual zeal, 'life', as they feed on him daily.

So we can draw up a few more conclusions.

4. **The Christian daily abides in Christ**. He reminds himself that Jesus has died for him; Jesus is alive in him; Jesus is interceding for him. He is **already** in Christ. (You have to be in a certain position before you can **stay** or 'abide' there.) It is not a great struggle; it is simply to remind oneself as to where you are and enjoy the fact that you are there. You simply enjoy staying in the position that has been given you.

Here is the great secret of godliness: beginning every day by deliberately feeding on the person of Jesus.

I personally have found it helpful to start every day by singing a little chorus that is about the resurrection.

Jesus is alive
Jesus is alive
His is the blood that ransoms me
His is the power that sets me free
He is the one that I shall see
For Jesus is alive.

I am not even sure where this comes from or whether I have the words right (I think not), but there is nothing that gives me more liberty every day than these simple words of a simple song.

Then you go deliberately, consciously into the presence of Jesus. The doorway is open. The blood of Jesus in heaven keeps the doorway into his presence permanently open. You simply walk through it by faith.

I have not given any rules or regulations in this chapter. There aren't any! I am not bothered about precisely how you do this – as long as you do it! Unless you will eat of Jesus, you will have no energy, no liveliness, none of the joy of the Lord which is your strength. To come down to the nitty-gritty, there is nothing more important than this. There will be no holiness without this.

This is what all the song-writers write about: Temptations lose their power when Thou art nigh!

Chapter 13

Receiving God's Word

We have seen our position in Christ; we know that we have the power of the Holy Spirit; and in Jesus we have fellowship with our heavenly Father every day.

What happens next is that God will speak to us through his Word. This can happen in different ways. It could be through a direct word from God, as when the Spirit said to Philip 'Approach that chariot and go up to it' (Acts 8:29). It was not a verse of Scripture that came to Philip; it was a direct word from God. Or it could be that God will use another Christian to speak to you. Maybe a few sentences as someone is preaching or ministering in a Christian gathering will be strikingly appropriate to your own situation; the words grip you as you hear them; you know it is a word from God. Or someone may share something with you privately which you know is from the Lord.

When the Bible says we are sanctified by God's Word (e.g. John 17:17; Ephesians 5:26; Psalm 119:9) what exactly is this 'Word of God'? It is not precisely the Bible or the New Testament. True, it amounts to that in the end, yet when the words recorded in John 17:17 were spoken, the New Testament did not exist. The 'Word of God' is the whole message of God's salvation; it is 'the truth'; it is 'the whole plan of God' (Acts 20:27). It came mainly as prediction in the ministry of Moses, in the Old Testament prophets and in the Old Testament wisdom writers. It came in fullness in the ministry of Jesus, whose teaching is called 'the Word' (Mark 2:2; 4:33). Through the apostles and prophets of the first generation of the Church 'the Word' reached its fullest form. Jesus had many things to say to his Church (John 16:12–15) and he said them through his apostles, beginning immediately after the day of Pentecost. In due course it was embodied in what we call 'the Bible' in its original languages, available to most people in translated form. It is this 'Word of God', coming to us in many ways but most clearly and definitively in the written Scriptures, that will change and mould our lives. The written form of the Word of God is its most reliable form. All other ways in which God speaks to us have to be checked. Inner voices or dreams or visions have to be carefully checked. One should not casually or unthinkingly act upon them. Churches that are too heavily dependent on these lesser forms of God's Word tend to become slightly eccentric – if not something worse! Although the idea of God giving revelations is entirely acceptable and biblical, no modern revelation can give a new teaching. The greatest church leader cannot propound a new doctrine. Although the modern concept of 'apostolic ministry' is a good one, in my opinion. (To put it at its lowest, it is better to have leaders of spiritual movements with the gift of mobilising others, than denominational committees and hierarchy who never seem to have such a gift!) Yet the greatest church leader cannot propound a new doctrine. All of us are dependent ultimately on the written Scripture.

A few verses in the letter to James will help us. James tells us that temptation does not come from God (James 1:13–16). What does come from God is the new birth (James 1:17). It is the fact that we have new life within us that enables us to be able to resist sin (James 1:18). But how does it work in practice? James tells us: He asks us to receive God's work with meekness; that will save us from sin.

First of all we are to be **eager to listen**. In the context of what James is saying this surely means 'Eager to listen to God's voice.' He has just referred to the 'word of truth'

(1:18) and will repeatedly refer to 'the word ... the word ... the word ... the perfect law' (1:21, 22, 23, 25). The secret of godliness is to be eager to hear God's voice.

Then James asks us **not to get angry with God's word when it comes to us**. In the context of what James is saying 'slow to speak and slow to become angry' refers to the way in which we react when God speaks to us. Sometimes when a word comes to us that rebukes us our instinct is to protest, to get angry and to start arguing back. But James says: Don't get angry when God speaks to you. Don't speak back too quickly.

Then we are told to **receive with meekness the implanted word**. When we hear God's voice we are to receive what he has to say. We do so with meekness, without defending ourselves, without arguing back against God. The word we receive is the 'implanted' word. What God has to say to us is not only **outside** of us embodied in the Scriptures. It is also **inside** us as well. When God gave us new birth, he planted his saving word in our hearts. His sheep hear his voice (John 10:16); they are taught of God; they hear and learn from the Father (John 6:45). The Christian is 'clean because of the word which Jesus has spoken' (John 15:3); an inward washing takes place as Jesus speaks to him. Why does the word need to be 'received' if it has already been 'implanted'? Because there is a difference between the implanted word and responding to the implanted word. Jesus said 'If you know these things [the first "if"] blessed are you if you do these things [the second "if"].' Some people do not 'know these things'. Some people do 'know these things' but do not do them. Some people both know and do. The stage where the Christian has been 'born again' is the stage where he knows. But there is a stage further on; he has to do, to respond, to receive deliberately and meekly, what God says to him.

As I say, the word of God can come in many forms. The way of speeding up the process is to turn regularly and persistently to God's **written** Word. This is what Jesus did. It is obvious that Jesus' mind was saturated with the written

Scriptures of the Old Testament. Although he was the Son
of God, although he possessed the Spirit without measure,
although he was directly given teaching from the Father,
yet he still felt the need to read and know the Scriptures of
the Old Testament. Someone has estimated that in ten
percent of Jesus' daily conversation he was quoting Old
Testament Scripture.[1] He knows its historical narratives; he
quotes it against the devil when being tempted; he reasons
with his enemies out of the Scriptures. He rebukes these
'theologians' of his day 'You do not know the Scriptures'
(Matthew 22:29). He asks them 'Have you not read...?'
(Matthew 22:31). The apostles held the same view. Paul
says to Timothy (2 Timothy 3:14–17): You have known the
written Scriptures since your earliest days. The people you
know so well as consistent godly people were people who
taught you the Scriptures. Now you be like them. These
writings are 'sacred' writings; they are 'God-breathed'.
They will teach you; they will rebuke you when you go
wrong; they will correct you and put you back on the right
path again; they will train you for service and ministry.
When God is speaking to you through these Scriptures you
are adequately equipped for the work God is calling you to.
The longest psalm, Psalm 119, is full of the same theme.
'How shall the young man cleanse his way?' asks the psalm-
writer, and answers his own question: 'By taking heed
according to your word.' The blessed person is the person
who meditates day and night on the 'torah', the personal
written 'teaching' of his heavenly Father.

So what then is the pathway of godliness? Amongst other
things it involves Bible-reading. Every Christian should
know what it is to study the Word of God, with concentra-
tion, with patience, in good slabs of time as well as in
hurried snatched moments. We need to have time daily
when we pore over the pages of God's word giving quality-
time to thought, meditation, prayerful questioning. We
need to be hearing from God – daily, learning new things –
daily, having old truths come back to us again – daily. We
need to ponder its words, its sentences. We need to stand

back and view large sections of Scripture; then we need to put small sections under the microscope.

In all of this we need to have a deep-seated hatred of any purely intellectual or detached view of Scripture. We are not interested in doctrine for its own sake. That was the fatal mistake of the Pharisees. 'You search the Scriptures,' said Jesus to the Pharisees, 'because you think that in them you have eternal life. Yet you will not come to me that you may have life.' Those learned scholars studied the Word of God in precisely the way I have just suggested. But they did it with a wrong spirit. They somehow felt their learned theology would give them eternal life. They said they were praying for the Messiah to come, but when he stood before their very eyes, they could not recognize him. With all their great Bible-knowledge they would not come to Jesus for life.

We are to 'meditate day and night' upon our heavenly father's teaching. But we do it in a very distinctive way. As we pore over every line we are breathing out the hunger of our heart, 'Lord speak to me. Grant that I may know that your Spirit is showing me these things. Lord I want to live this way, according to these very lines that I am reading.' It is good to have some kind of system in hearing from God in this way, and yet to my mind it has to be a very flexible system. I have never liked the 'through the Bible in a year' systems, and even less do I like those that are more ambitious. To my mind they are a bondage. I get interested in the first verse of the first chapter they want me to read and an hour later I have got no further. I get behind within a week and end up like Martin Luther when he was a Catholic monk; he risked his health and sanity trying to catch up with his devotional 'arrears'!

My way is this: I have a mixed-up order of the books of the Bible,[2] which I work through reading as much or as little as I feel is right, each day. Sometimes I might read ten chapters, sometimes I might spend hours on a verse. But I always carry on the next day where I left off the previous day. I find it is flexible, satisfying. If one does skip a day –

but I rarely do – it does not matter very much. One of my daughters complains my system is not sufficiently disciplined, but I am unrepentant. I love it, have used it for the last 13 years with great delight and will no doubt stick to it until I go to heaven. Maybe one day I'll write a legalistic version for my daughter – with passages specified for particular dates of the year – but personally I enjoy my freedom!

This kind of daily meditation might go something like this. Every day one spends time to talk to our heavenly Father. But in addition one finds a part of the day specially for God's written Word. You read through a section, asking God to speak to you clearly. God will hear you – but maybe in a way that is quite surprising. Sometimes quite an 'odd' angle of thought gives you the answer to some prayer or problem you have been wrestling with. I was struggling a few days ago with something that was a burden and concern to me. Late at night, about 11.30 pm, I was in the Word of God, in a section of my system that works through Psalms 1–18; I was in Psalm 2. As I was reading I saw verse 8 in a new light: 'Ask of me and I will surely give....' I knew it was ultimately about Jesus asking the Father for the kingdom that he was to rule in. But I was gripped by the principle: even Jesus did not get his kingdom without asking. I knew what God was saying to me: 'You will have to do some more asking. Ask and I will give it to you...'

I remember where I was a year ago. I was in India at the time, and (although I did not realize exactly what the problem was) I was exceedingly ill. I was wondering whether God was going to take me to heaven. At that time I was reading my system at two points at two different times of the day, at one point for myself, at another point I was writing some notes on a book of Scripture for a friend. One of my readings was in Philippians. I opened my Bible to carry on reading where I had left off the previous day, and to scribble some notes. It was Philippians 1. 'To me to live is Christ, and to die is gain.' I felt so ill. 'Wow, that's for me!' I thought. 'I'll be in heaven soon!' It made me turn to the Lord. Was I willing to lose my life preaching in a rural village in India? But then I read on: '...yet to remain on in the flesh is more necessary.' I came to believe **that** was the bit the Lord was laying on my heart. It enabled me to hold on for another week before I got back to Nairobi, back to a doctor, to discover I had been walking around with typhoid for a fortnight!

A few months later I was being a bit self-willed and impatient. God rebuked me as I read about John the Baptist 'A person can have **nothing**,' God said to me, 'unless it is given to him from above' (John 3:27).

At another point I was reading of the miracle in 2 Kings 6:1–7 and dipping into A.W. Pink's commentary on those verses. God spoke to me again about something I felt had sunk to the bottom of my life. 'Tell Jesus the heavenly Elisha about the sunken axe-head that concerns you,' God said to me. 'He will make it float again.'

God speaks again and again in these ways. Sometimes he rebukes severely in ways I would not like to share with anyone! Sometimes he lays something gigantic upon us and demands that we do it. But much of the time His words are not heavy. They are just encouragements when one is weary, props to faith when one is doubtful, slaps on the wrist when one is careless, helps along the way, challenges to love and kindness towards others, calls to prayer and fasting, invitations to worship, calls to ministry or particular tasks.

But it is not always something personal and local that God lays upon our hearts. Sometimes it is a glimpse of the majesty of God. Jonathan Edwards could say 'Sometimes, only mentioning a single word caused my heart to burn within me; or only seeing the name of Christ, or the name of some attribute of God.' Sometimes God showed him 'the excellent fullness of Christ, and his meetness and suitableness as a Saviour.'[3]

One thing is sure: this is the pathway of godliness. Receive with meekness the implanted Word; it is able to save our lives from the damage of sin, able to shape us so that we steadily become more like Jesus.

Endnotes

(1) See H. Rimmer, *Internal Evidences of Inspiration*, Eerdmans, 1938, p. 227 cited in R.P. Lightner, *The Saviour and the Scriptures*, Presbyterian & Reformed, 1966, p. 28.

(2) The order I use is Genesis, Matthew, Joshua, Romans, Isaiah, Proverbs, Hebrews, Psalms 1–18, Hosea, Psalms 19–25, Joel, Psalms 26–33, 1 Corinthians, Jeremiah, James, Psalms 34–39, Exodus, John, Judges, Song of Songs, Psalms 40–47, Ruth, 1 Peter, Lamentations, Psalms 48–55, Ecclesiastes, 2 Peter, Psalms 56–64, 2 Corinthians, Esther, Daniel, Psalms 65–70, 1 John, Psalms 71–77, Mark, Ezra, 2 John, Psalms 78–81, 3 John, Jude, Psalms 82–89, 1 Samuel, Galatians, Nehemiah, Psalms 90–104, Ephesians, Psalms 105–108, Luke, Philippians, Ezekiel, 1 Chronicles, Colossians, Psalms 109–118, Numbers, 2 Samuel, 1 Thessalonians, Job, Amos, Psalm 119, 2 Thessalonians, Obadiah, 1 Kings, Jonah, Pslms 120–132, 1 Timothy, Micah, Nahum, Habakkuk, Psalms 133–141, Deuteronomy, Acts, 2 Kings, 2 Timothy, Zephaniah, Haggai, Titus, Zechariah, Malachi, Philemon, 2 Chronicles, Psalms 142–150, Revelation.

(3) *The Works of Jonathan Edwards*, Banner of Truth, 1974, vol. 1, p. xlvii.

PART THREE

How – Helps and Hints

Chapter 14

The Law of Liberty

One might want to ask the question: are there any guide-lines in the life of holiness? We are not under the law of Moses with its circumcision and its law about holy foods and holy days and so on. We are not precisely under the ten commandments, although we 'fulfil' the law by walking in the Spirit. Certainly no one keeps the Sabbath in its Mosaic form. And eight of the other nine commandments are actually too low a level for the Christian, taken as they stand. It is actually the tenth command ('you shall not covet') that really gets us!

What is the guideline for the Christian? It is what James calls 'the law of liberty'. What is this 'law of liberty'?

It is not the Mosaic law. James does not mention the ten commandments or anything that is distinctive to the Mosaic law. But what he does do (following Jesus) is this: he picks out from a very obscure part of the Mosaic law one sentence, 'Love your neighbour as yourself' and he makes that the law of liberty for the Christian or what he calls 'the royal law'.

What then is this 'law of liberty' and why is it called a 'law of liberty'?

One reason it is a 'law of liberty' is: it begins by providing forgiveness. Have you ever heard of a law that begins by providing forgiveness for breaches of its demands? But that is precisely what the gospel of Jesus does. Think of the story of the woman caught in adultery. The Jewish leaders

89

who brought her to Jesus wanted to apply the Mosaic law. The penalty for adultery in the Mosaic law was that she be stoned to death. What does Jesus say? 'Neither do I condemn you; go your way; from now on don't sin any longer' (John 8:11). Notice the order. It is not 'Don't sin any longer, and then I will not condemn you.' It **starts** by saying 'I am not condemning you. And **then** Jesus' requirement is 'Don't sin any longer.' The law of liberty **begins** by telling us: all manner of sins shall be forgiven. John writes: 'I am writing these things to you so that you don't sin, but **if any person does sin**, we have an advocate with the Father Jesus Christ the righteous and he is the sacrifice for our sins' (1 John 2:1–2). What liberty! We must not sin, but when we do there is forgiveness. A law of liberty indeed! Too good to be true, in the eyes of many.

The law of Jesus is a law of liberty because Jesus so works in us that his yoke is light and his burden is easy. This too is hard for many to believe, but Jesus says it with lucid plainness (Matthew 11:28–30). True, the will of God often seems hard. Jesus found the will of God so difficult he sweated drops of blood and asked that if there was any other way, please, might he not go the other way (Luke 22:41–44)? But actually when we submit at that point the will of God turns out to be easy after all! The moment you surrender to Jesus' will for your life, such grace is given to us that it is no longer so agonizing after all. It is so liberating. Jesus promises he will never put upon us a burden too great for us to bear (1 Corinthians 10:13).

The law of the kingdom is a law of liberty because Jesus is asking us to **want** to follow him. 'If anyone **wants** to come after me...', he says. There was nothing like that in the Mosaic law. Under the Mosaic law the demands were laid upon you whether you wanted them or not! But Jesus will lead you by the Spirit in such a way that we **want** to be like him. When we are walking in the paths of discipleship we are getting what we **want**. It is not a burden; it is liberty! There is a great desire in our hearts to be all that God wants us to be. We get to know that his will is rewarding, enriching, fulfilling.

Jesus' requirement is a 'law of liberty' because we are in fact given a great deal of liberty. God works in us along the lines of the way we are made. Often when we ask God 'Lord, what do you want me to do for you?', he answers 'Well, what do you want to do for me?' God loves us to want to serve him and then he gives us what we want. Commit your way unto him, says the Psalmist, and he will give you the desires of your heart (Psalm 37:4). However, when you commit your way unto God, he can trust you enough to give you the desires of your heart. The desires of your heart will be good but they will also flow along the channel of the way you are made and the gifts that you have. When you find God's call for your life, it is liberty! It fits the way you are made. It is being given the desires of your heart. Happiness is being in the will of God.

Jesus' requirement is a 'law of liberty' because it all boils down to one supreme thing: loving everyone everywhere. I once counted the number of verses in the books of Exodus to Deuteronomy that could be called legislation; there were over two thousand. To this day, Jewish scholars reckon they amount to 613 laws. The Jew (says a modern Jewish rabbi) 'has a mental filing cabinet for all he learns and six-hundred and thirteen concepts to think about at all times.'[1] It includes such things as not walking outside the city limits on a Saturday (see Exodus 16:29), giving half a shekel annually (see Exodus 30:13), not eating fruit from a tree during its first three years (see Leviticus 19:23) and not eating fresh grapes (see Numbers 6:3)! But Jesus has a better way of holiness than that!

In the law itself the Ten Commandments is the summary of the two thousand or so detailed requirements. The Mosaic law could be reduced to ten basic 'words' (Exodus 34:28).

Jesus could say that the intent of the law could be reduced to two: loving God and loving our neighbour (Mark 12:29–31).

But the 'law of liberty' actually reduces the will of God to one point: the law of love. It might come as a surprise that the one chosen (from Leviticus 19) is 'Love your neighbour.' 'Surely' – you might say – 'if the law is to be reduced to one principle, it is love **of God** that ought to be chosen as the one.' No, not at all! The reason why love of our neighbour is the one is that it is only too easy for us to fool ourselves that we are loving God but not so easy to delude ourselves into thinking we are loving our neighbour. John put it like this: 'If anyone says "I love God" and yet hates his or her brother, he is a liar. For the person who does not love his brother, whom he has seen, cannot be loving God whom he has not seen' (1 John 4:20). We do not see God, literally. It is too easy to persuade ourselves that we are loving God. But when it comes to a brother or sister in Jesus, it is a different matter. There he is, right before us. We can see him. If we are in a bad relationship with him it is rather more difficult to pretend that things are other than what they are. The more crucial test is not 'do I love God?' – where I can convince myself that I do, but 'do I love my fellow Christian?' – where it is not so easy for me to deceive myself.

So the one thing to focus on is Christian love, seeing things from the other person's point of view (Matthew 7:12). Being like Jesus to him. Making him or her feel forgiven, wanted, valued, encouraged. That is the law of liberty!

It might be asked: is not this 'law of liberty' too vague? No! It is definite. It is not a hidebound codified rulebook of ethics, but it **can** be expressed in words. Paul and other New Testament writers can talk about what the leading of the Spirit is. They can put it into propositions. This is what the lengthy exhortations of the New Testament are (in Ephesians 4–6, Romans 12–15, and elsewhere). It sometimes happened in New Testament times that people would go into error or start saying or doing crazy things and blaming it on to the 'leading of the Spirit'. So Paul would write these New Testament letters to correct them and get them on to right lines again. But he was not expounding the Mosaic law! He was putting into his own words the kind of life that he knows the Spirit will lead us into. There was nothing vague about it. Paul knew precisely how the Spirit would be leading, and he knew that people who committed immorality (1 Corinthians) or said that the second coming of Jesus would be tomorrow morning (1, 2 Thessalonians) or that we should get circumcised (Galatians) were mistaken and that their views were **not** the leading of the Spirit.

Another question asked is: could this 'law of liberty' not be misused? Yes! You can twist any doctrine. Grace can be twisted into licentiousness (Jude 4). But don't develop a spirit of fear. We have not been given a spirit of fear, but we have been given the Spirit of love and of power and of good judgement (2 Timothy 1:7). Don't throw out the baby with the bath water. The bath water is licentiousness and indiscipline; throw it out. But the baby is the amazing grace of God. Hold on to the baby! Is there any check on the 'law of liberty'? Yes. First of all, you have a conscience. You are to 'hold faith and a good conscience' (1 Timothy 1:19; see also 1:5; 3:9; 2 Timothy 1:3). Your conscience is not infallible. It could be too easy-going or it could be too strict. But it will help you, and you will grow in your understanding. When you are making a mistake your conscience will hold you back.

Secondly, there is such a thing as the forbidding of the Spirit. When Paul felt he wanted to go to Bithynia and was about to move, he felt forbidden and he held back (Acts 16:7).

Thirdly, you may follow Jesus' test: by their fruits you shall know them. Does legalism lead into liberty and boldness and energetic Christian love? Or is the godly life a matter of honestly and conscientiously following the 'law of liberty'. The legalism of the Galatians led to their 'biting and devouring' one another (Galatians 5:15). By their fruits you shall know them.

Also – a surprising twist in the Bible's way of putting things – when you walk in the Spirit you 'fulfil' the law! I did not say you are 'under' the law. You are 'under grace' (Romans 6:14). But when you are 'under grace' you end up fulfilling what the law was driving at all the time. The leading of the Spirit is more delicate, more gentle, yet more powerful than the Mosaic law. The Mosaic law took into account hardness of heart (Matthew 19:8) but the leading of the Spirit takes into account the softness of heart that is given to the Christian and that he should protect (Hebrews 3:12). For God has given us not a heart of stone but 'a heart of flesh' (Ezekiel 36:26) that is sensitive to him.

When we live this way we 'fulfil the law'. The life of love does not lead into sin. Think about Romans 13:8–10. The various commands of the law, 'You shall not commit adultery', 'You shall not murder', 'You shall not steal' – and if there be any other commandment – it is all brought together in this **one** point: 'you shall love your neighbour as yourself'. The 'law of liberty' will never lead you into sin. But the Spirit will lead you into a life of love, and that will bring you into purity, gentleness, ease and relaxation with people. The Spirit will lead you into prayer and intercession for others. You will pray for your enemies. You will do good to those who despitefully use you. The Spirit will lead you beyond the Mosaic law, and yet you will fulfil the Mosaic law. You will get to a level of righteousness that exceeds anything scribes and Pharisees think of, and you will enjoy the blessings of God's kingdom.

Endnote

(1) Rabbi Alon I. Tolwin, *The 613 Mitzvos: A Study Guide*, Old City Press, Jerusalem, 1983, p. 2.

Chapter 15

Maintaining Our Joy

One key to help in the godly life is to keep rejoicing! The joy of the Lord is our strength (Nehemiah 8:10). A depressed Christian is a vulnerable Christian. We are urged to rejoice at all times (Psalm 33:1; 1 Thessalonians 5:16; Philippians 4:4).

Let us think of the different kinds of joy and the different ways in which we are to rejoice in our Lord.

(1) There is **the joy of facing life realistically and contentedly**. This is a major theme of the book of Ecclesiastes. The purpose of the book of Ecclesiastes is, amongst other things, to get us to face life as it really is. This world is a fallen place, 'subject unto vanity' (Romans 8:20; Ecclesiastes 1:2). Ecclesiastes persistently calls us to a life of faith, joy and contentment.

The answer to the 'futility' of life, according to 'the Preacher', is to take life day by day from the hand of God. What does it mean practically? It means that we refuse panic or vexation or anxiety. 'Remove vexation from your heart,' says the wise man (Ecclesiastes 11:10). He continues: 'and put away pain from your body.' It means that we are sensible in taking care of ourselves physically. And we live to please God. 'To the person who pleases him, God gives wisdom and knowledge and joy' (Ecclesiastes 2:26). It means that we trust in God to provide for us, to enable us to 'eat and drink and tell himself that his labour is good' (Ecclesiastes 2:24). We trust in the timing of God:

95

'He has made everything beautiful in its time' (Ecclesiastes 3:11). I say to God: 'My times are in your hands' (Psalm 31:15). We trust in the sovereignty of God (Ecclesiastes 3:14). We believe that he works effectively. 'Everything God does will remain for ever.' We believe that he works completely and leaves nothing out. 'There is nothing to add to it and nothing to take from it.' We believe that everything he does is purposeful; it is 'so that men and women should fear him.'

In other words, Ecclesiastes calls us to contentment, to liberty of conscience in enjoying God's world. The world is a futile place, but to take life day-by-day from the hand of God is the remedy. 'Everything created by God is good, and nothing is to be rejected if it is received with thanksgiving' (1 Timothy 4:4). 'Happy is he who does not condemn himself...', says Paul. In context, he is referring to being a meat-eater rather than a vegetarian. But the principle may be widened. Happy is he who enjoys God's world, who likes the sunshine and physical relaxation, who can enjoy good music and good friendships. Happy is he who knows that God approves of him. 'He who doubts is condemned ... whatever is not of faith is sin.'

I could call this 'ordinary' joy. It is the joy that comes from having a 'strong' conscience, where one does not fall easily into self-condemnation or narrowness or fear of enjoying God's world.

This has a major impact upon our holiness. A narrow legalistic Christian will find himself prone to sin, especially prone to grumbling and criticism. Happy is he who does not condemn himself in what he approves.

(2) Then there is **the joy that comes by keeping free from introspection**. This is more of a problem to some people than to others. But even the most extrovert have their introspective moments.

How do we keep free from introspection? Know that Jesus died for you! It is all over the Bible: Jesus died for everyone. He loved the world (John 3:16); he died 'not for our sins only, but also for the sins of the whole world' (1 John 2:2). And that includes you!

Know that you have been released from everything that might condemn you. You have 'died to sin' (Romans 6). Sin can never condemn you (Romans 8:1). Don't concentrate on trying to deliver yourself from the reasons for your feeling condemned. Just know that you are not condemned! Your freedom from condemnation comes at the **beginning** of your relationship with God; it does not arrive when you get to a certain level of maturity. It is not that you are struggling to reach a certain level of godliness and consistency and when you get there you will be uncondemned. No! If you believe in Jesus you are uncondemned now! And Jesus is touched with the feeling of your weaknesses (Hebrews 4:15). The things that you feel ashamed of and that make you feel rejected arouse Jesus' sympathy. Jesus is touched by them. If Jesus is your Saviour 'keep yourself in the love of God' (Jude 21). Do not let yourself feel condemned. Find joy in believing (Romans 15:13).

(3) The next thing we must mention is **the joy of God's promises**. He is a very present help in trouble (Psalm 46:1). He promises to provide for our needs (Philippians 4:19). He argues with us, persuading us not to worry (Matthew 6:25–34). He promises to work everything together for us. He promises never to leave us. Indeed there are hundreds and thousands of promises in the Bible. Every one of them finds their 'Yes!' in Jesus (2 Corinthians 1:18–20). Will Jesus really provide for me (Philippians 4:19)? Yes! Yes! Of course He will. Will Jesus really work everything together for good in my life (Romans 8:28)? If you love him ('to them that love God'), He will. Yes! Yes! All of the promises of God find their 'Yes' in him. What we have to do is 'utter the Amen'. We have to say 'If God has promised then I am going to believe it.' He never lies. This is the secret of joy and liberty.

(4) **Then there is the joy of answered prayer.** How wonderful it is when God hears our praying. Many will say 'But he does not seem to hear me!' I reply: Why doesn't he? He is willing to. Go to him in the name of Jesus. Seek first his kingdom before anything else. Put every real need before

him. Don't ask for things that are sinful. Be willing for him to delay purely personal requests and shape them up to his will before he answers them. But he is a God who hears prayer. Don't be anxious about anything (Philippians 4:6–7). Come to him with prayer – general praise and worship and prayer about his kingdom and his will. Come to him with supplication, casting yourself upon his mercy. Come to him with thanksgiving. And in that setting put your requests to him. He will give you peace immediately, and it is very likely that he will hear your request. Certainly he will meet your need in one way or another. There is no joy like the joy of leaning on God in this way. You will discover the amazing faithfulness of God.

(5) Then I must mention **the joy of obedience**. Jesus says if we keep his commandments we shall abide in his love; his joy will be in us and our joy will be full (John 15:11). There is great joy that comes when we are obedient to Jesus. The heart and centre of everything Jesus wants for us is love. And there is great joy in love. That is why the fruit of the Spirit is said to be 'love, joy...', and so on. Why does Paul put love first? Because it is first. (But what immediately follows is joy, peace, patience, and the rest of the fruit of the Spirit). Paul knew what he was doing when he put love first. There can never be joy without love. There can never be peace without love. If we put obedience first, the obedience that will involve loving everyone everywhere, joy will follow. If we take the words that God speaks to us and 'eat' them (Jeremiah 15:16), that is 'take them into our very life and get strength from them,' living on God's words to us will become the 'joy and delight of my heart.' God will become 'God my exceeding joy' (Psalm 43:4).

(6) We happen to learn to **insist on rejoicing no matter what happens to us**. Habakkuk lived in difficult days, but he ends his prophecy telling us that he is determined to rejoice in God no matter what happens (Habakkuk 3:17, 18), whether the fig tree blossoms or not! It does not matter whether there is a good harvest or there 'is no fruit on the vines.' Though the olives fail, though the fields produce no

food, though the animals on the farm all perish, it makes no difference. 'I will rejoice in the LORD,' says Habakkuk. Jesus lived that way as well. Even when he was on the cross it was 'because of the joy that was set before him' that he 'endured the cross despising the shame' (Hebrews 12:2). Jesus had the oil of gladness above his fellows, the angels (Psalm 45:7; Hebrews 1:9). The apostle Paul lived in the same way. He was sorrowful in many trials and testings yet always rejoicing (2 Corinthians 6:10). He was able to sing in prison (Acts 16:25), after he had been arrested for preaching about Jesus.

We are urged to rejoice. It is something that is commanded! It is not purely a matter of letting some emotion overwhelm us. We don't simply sit back and wait for the joy of the Lord to come. Remember how the Psalmist argues with himself: 'Why are you in despair, O my soul?' (Psalm 42:5). Notice he is talking to himself! 'Hey, soul!' he says. 'What is the matter with you? What are you doing moping and grumbling in that way? Don't you believe in God, the living, mighty God?' Hope in God! Be confident that you will be rejoicing in him soon. Start now! He will command his loving kindness in the daytime. Like the apostle Paul, you will find he will give you a song in the night-time. Put all your trust in God, refuse to be miserable! Any moment now you will be praising him again, so you may as well start now (Psalm 42, throughout).

The joy of the Lord can be lost by serious sin. Even then it is possible to get it back. David did the most awful things and apparently lost his joy in God. But at least he knew what to do about it. He went back to God and pleaded that God would give it back to him (Psalm 51:12). Make sure you maintain your joy; the joy of the Lord is your strength.

Chapter 16

Resisting Temptation

The Christians to whom the letter of James was written were what we would call 'respectable backsliders'. They were moral people but they were guilty of sins of discrimination, quarrelsomeness and lack of love. The letter to James is, amongst other things, a guide to holiness and to spiritual restoration. One thing they needed to know was how to face various trials and temptations. How we handle temptation determines how great we are as godly men and women.

What James does in James 1:13–17 is simply to describe what happens when we are tempted. The first thing he wants us to know is that temptation does not come from God. Sometimes a temptation can seem so 'right'. Think about Jonah. When he wanted to run away from God everything was there for him. There was the ship, conveniently sailing in the opposite direction from Nineveh. The sailors were willing to take Jonah on board; everything was so 'providential'. It is often this way when we are tempted; some sin or mistaken decision can seem so right. We can even feel that we are being 'guided' when we are walking into the pathways of sin. James says 'Don't be fooled. God can never want us to do anything that he has revealed is sin. It is impossible. God cannot be persuaded to support you when you sin, and certainly never entices anyone into sin.'

No, temptation comes from within. What James does to help us is to describe the stages by which we go down into sin. There are five of them: temptation, what he calls 'conception', then the sin itself, then the growth of sin, then the consequence of sin, death.

Stage number one is when a desire is pulling at us. This is our difficulty. Often our desires get out of control. It may be our desire for glory, the desire to feel superior, the desire to be admired, for self-esteem, for security, for possessions, for independence from God rather than security in God. It may be our self-will, our sexuality, our pride. These desires are within us. We must be aware of them, and know that they are a permanent tug within us in the direction of sin. However temptation is not itself sin. We must not get into the bondage of feeling condemned every time some desire rises within our hearts.

Some people develop over-sensitive consciences. The Romans thought they had to be vegetarians (Romans 14:2). The Corinthians were fearful of eating meat bought at a butcher's shop (1 Corinthians 10:25). Some had been open to legalists who forbade marriage (1 Timothy 4:3–4). No, our desires and inclinations are not necessarily sin in themselves, although when they run out of control they can lead us into sin. There is the desire to deceive. There is the passionate longing to put someone down, as when Haman (after what he thought was a good day) found his day ruined by meeting Mordecai (Esther 5:9). There is consuming sexual desire like Ammon's frustration because he could not have his half-sister Tamar (2 Samuel 13:2). There is desire for possessions or money or land or security, like Ahab when he lay depressed and miserable on his bed because he could not get what he wanted. There is the desire for revenge, the desire to be self-righteous, the desire to dominate.

Stage number two is when desire 'conceives'. This is when you welcome the suggestion that your desires are putting to you. At this point sin catches hold of us and says 'Come with me' (like the immoral woman of Proverbs 7:13–15). At this point we have not yet sinned. If we back out at the last moment, all is well. We can still be like Joseph and run for our lives when sin – or its representative – takes hold of us and says 'Come with me' (Genesis 39:12). Joseph had not sinned when he fled from Potiphar's wife. Sometimes we discover what it is to escape when we are just about to do something foolish.

This is the heart of temptation. The trouble is that unless you are rejoicing in the Lord and committed to God, at the point where sin is trying to catch hold of you, temptation produces a kind of blindness. We can be extraordinarily foolish, passionately wanting something which we shall see is wrong a few seconds after our fall. A strange blindness comes down upon us when we are tempted. A total commitment **in advance** to God and his will can keep us at such a time. But our strength at that particular point depends on what we have been **before** that point. If Joseph had not been utterly committed to God **before** the advances of Potiphar's wife, I doubt whether he would have stood in the hour of temptation.

The third stage is that we actually sin. This is when you yield to the suggestion.

Stage number four is that sin grows. Once you have yielded to sin, it is likely to grasp at you again, and again, and again. Sin has a habit of growing. Whosoever commits sin is a slave of sin (John 8:34).

Stage number five is death: spiritual insensitivity, godlessness, living without the enjoyment of God's favour. It can happen even to the Christian. 'If you sow to the flesh' (says Paul to the Christians in Galatia) 'you will back from the flesh reap corruption.'

What does James want us to do about all of this? Why is it that James does not give us a list of things to do or ways in which we shall be protected from temptation? What he is doing is placing a lot of responsibility upon us. He tells us the stages of temptation so that we might recognize them and set ourselves to resist in the very beginning of the process.

What can we do? First, we must refuse to be deceived. Verse 16 is repeating verse 13. Second, we must know that

God gives good things. God will **only** give good things. It is alright to **want** things but God will only give what is good. He meets our needs. He provides food, clothing, companionship, love, shelter, safety, purpose for living. God hears prayer (Psalm 65:2, 9–13). He rewards us when we seek him (Hebrews 11:6). His grace is bigger than our sins (Romans 5:20). He cares for us (1 Peter 5:7). He promises to hear our prayers (Matthew 7:7, 8, 11; 21:22; John 14:14; 16:24). Every time we are tempted we are actually being gripped with the conviction that we shall somehow lose out if we do not get what we want. If we are gripped with the conviction that God is good to us, we need not fear that our desires will be unsatisfied. God has ways of satisfying us and of meeting all of our needs.

When we are tempted to steal it is because we are not sure that God will provide for us. When we are tempted into a wrong relationship it is because we fear God will not give us friendship and love. When we are tempted into sins of anxiety it is because we are not casting all of our cares upon him. The answer to temptation is to know that we need never fear. Every good thing is given to us by God. But God will only give what is good; he will never support our sins. We can trust him to meet our needs and to satisfy every longing of our heart in ways that are clean and pure.

We have already seen that God's supreme good gift from above is the new birth. It is that which enables us to respond to his Word.

The strange thing is: sometimes none of this seems to be very practical. We do get deceived! We **know** God gives good things. We know we ought to respond to God's Word. 'But,' I can hear you saying 'I still seem to give in to temptation. Why does not James say something more practical?' Because there is not anything more to say! There comes a point where you must accept responsibility. Cleanse yourself from every defilement of body and of spirit! (2 Corinthians 7:1). Resist the devil! (James 4:7). You say you cannot do it? If you know Jesus, you can! You can do all things through Christ who strengthens you (Philippians 4:13).

It is no good praying about it. Don't even pray about it. Do it! Let him who stole steal no more. 'What impractical advice!', you say. What is the good of saying to a compulsive thief 'Steal no more.' His very problem is that he can't seem to stop it. But Paul was writing to Christians. The Christian thief **can** stop it. Steal no more! The immoral Christian can stop. Be immoral no more.

It may be that at this point there is nothing I can say to you except: You have a divided will! You are born again. The Spirit is within you. You have died to sin. You are alive unto God. The Holy Spirit is within you to help you. Don't pray any more. Don't fast any more. Don't go to any more holiness meetings. Just sin no more! You tell me you can't do it? I tell you you can do it. Do you believe in the gospel or don't you? Do you believe in the power of the Spirit or don't you? Yield to the Spirit's promptings. You will suffer, maybe, when you break away from that sin. But accept the pain. Resist the sin. When you have resisted once, it gets a little easier. Resist the devil. James promises you; he will flee from you. Draw near to God. James promises you; God will draw near to you.

Chapter 17

Chastening

What would you say is the greatest stimulus to godliness? The Bible? The Holy Spirit? Christian fellowship? I could understand why any of these answers might be given. But from a certain viewpoint the greatest stimulus to holiness is God's chastening!

Hebrews chapter 12 is perhaps the fullest statement of the matter in the Bible. At that stage in his great letter the writer has said much to them about pressing on with the Lord. He has just been showing them (Hebrews chapter 11) that all of the great saints of the Old Testament lived by faith.

Now he wants them to live in the same way. He puts it to them in terms of a race. Imagine, he says, a race taking place in an arena. There is the crowd watching the race. There are the runners dressed in light clothing. There is great effort that the runners are making. There is the course along which they must run. There is the prize and the one who gives the prize. In Hebrews 12:1–2 the writer applies all of this to his Christian friends. There is the great crowd (with an 'r'), a crowd with so many people that they are like a cloud (with an 'l'), so many that they are just a grey mass. Who are they? They are the heroes of Hebrews chapter 11 telling us of their victory. They are shouting to us 'We made it! So can you.' The runners do not wear heavy clothing. When you are a runner you run in light clothes. So it is with the Christian. He puts off hindrances and sins. 'Hindrances' and 'sins' are not the same. 'Hindrances' are things that are not sinful in themselves yet they hinder our Christian race. They might include certain friendships, excessive concern about some pleasures, snobbishness about one's 'advantages', a concern not to look foolish, bitterness, protectiveness, cares, riches.

Then there is great effort required, and there is a definite course to be followed. It is the pathway of faith. Then there is the prize, and the giver of the prize, Jesus himself.

But he has to remind them: athletics has a tough side to it. There is some tough training for them if they are to achieve anything in this heavenly race. There is the tough training of the chastening of God.

What is 'chastening'? Three words are used in Hebrews chapter 12. Chastening is **discipline** (Hebrews 12:5), fatherly correction; it is **reproof** (Hebrews 12:5), rebuke, censure when we are going astray or about to go astray. It is **lashing** or **scourging** (Hebrews 12:6), painful experiences that makes us pull away from what we had been doing.

The author of Hebrews gives us a warning: we must be willing to face God's chastening. There are a number of matters that call for attention in his words.

1. **Chastening is something we tend to forget.** We tend to feel somehow that life is guaranteed to be easier if we know Jesus. This is a half-truth. The fact is we are told very clearly that we shall from time to time face the discipline of God. Jesus is the vine, we are the branches, and 'every branch that bears fruit he cleanses so that it may bear more fruit' (John 15:2).

2. **Chastening is part of God's fatherly care.** It is not necessary to think that God is rejecting us or condemning us when we experience chastening. Chastening is part of sonship. All the saints of God went through such painful experiences. Joseph was greatly used by God, but he suffered much first from his brothers, then from Potiphar's wife. Think of David, Abraham and Sarah, Job, Paul. They were all put through great perplexities and sufferings.

3. **Chastening is a proof of love.** What is love? Amongst

other things it is taking action when we see a need. Chastening works on the same principle. God sees a need of correction in us; it is love that is being shown when he takes action. Chastening is painful, but it is love which is at work.

The famous John 3:16 says 'God so loved the world that He gave His only Son so that whoever believes in Him should not perish but have everlasting life.' But we could write an analogous verse of our own! 'God so loved the church that he gives whatever chastening is needed, so that whoever receives it should not lose his inheritance but have everlasting reward.' Love is operating in both situations.

4. **Chastening does not go on for ever.** It sometimes feels as though it will. 'When will it end?' we say. But Hebrews 12:11 says 'At present, all discipline seems not enjoyable but painful. Later it yields the peaceable fruits of righteousness.' There is a 'present' and a 'later' in chastening. It will end.

5. **Chastening is inevitable for all Christians.** There is no way of escaping it. 'All are sharers' (Hebrews 12:8). To be without the experience of God's chastening would be a proof that we are not the children of God at all. When we experience God's hand powerfully administering rebuke it is a sign we are his children indeed.

6. **Chastening may be powerfully effective**. I did not say it *inevitably* will be effective; much depends on how we face it. But it can detach us from worldly ways; it can bring us to greater dependence on God. It makes God's promises more precious to us. It gets us to be more sympathetic to others. It reveals more of God to us. It strengthens our character, works patience and steadfastness and humility in us. Above all it increases our fellowship with Jesus.

Received in the right way it brings about life. 'Shall we not much more be submissive ... and then we shall live!' Chastening produces an increase of life. We have greater liveliness towards God.

How then should we receive God's chastening? Firstly, Hebrews 12:5 says we should not despise it. We should not try to shrug it off, ignore it, pretend we do not need it.

Secondly, we should not faint. 'Fainting' is falling into self-pity and despair. We must not lose hope when we go through trials and tribulations. God is not our enemy. The chastening will not go on for ever.

Thirdly, instead of despising our trials or fainting under them, we listen to the reproof, we submit to the discipline, we allow the painful lashing to produce in us a fear of going near anything that displeases God. Hebrews 12:9 talks about 'submitting'. Chastening is reasonable and necessary. It is part of the Father–Son relationship. Hebrews 12:12–13 gets down to some details. We lift our drooping hands: we refuse to let our hands hang loose in despair and we get ready for action, for service. Chastening is God's preparation for serving him in holiness and righteousness. We strengthen our weak knees. We get ready to walk straight without stumbling. If there have been things in our lives that make us walk stumblingly we deal with them. We straighten out our paths.

Then the writer tells us what will happen: there will be healing. Our life begins to get to be the way it ought to be. We go after holiness and peace with all people: holiness towards God, peaceableness towards people.

The writer follows up his words with a warning about what will happen if we do not allow God to deal with us in this way. He says 'Don't be like Esau.' Esau is an illustration of a believer who does not bother about holiness. He grew up in a believing family. He claimed to believe all that Abraham believed. He was no **less** godly than Jacob – but then there was nothing very godly about Jacob to begin with!

But Esau had no interest in the spiritual blessings that were available to him through the promises of God. He became bitter, he spread defilement in the family, he was careless in his relationship with the opposite sex. He put earthly pleasures before the inheritance he could have had. Eventually he lost his inheritance altogether and Jacob took an oath that it should not be his (Genesis 27:27–29).

The epistle to the Hebrews applies all of this to its

readers. If they are careless about accepting the chastening of God and being led in this powerful way into holiness and peace with all people, if they 'neglect such a great salvation' (Hebrews 2:3), how will they escape God's displeasure? The lessons of Esau's life apply to them. Let them beware of missing the experience of God's grace leading them into the godly life (Hebrews 12:15). Let them avoid at all costs the bitterness of spirit that will block the flow of blessing. Let them avoid spreading any kind of defilement in the fellowship of the Christians (12:15). Let them steer clear of immorality or anything approaching it. Let them beware of godlessness, a creeping indifference and hardness of heart that leads them to 'fall away from the living God' (Hebrews 3:12).

If God should take an 'oath of wrath' and swear that the inheritance is lost, the Christian would then be in the position of Esau, a person lined up for inheritance but one who irretrievably lost it. Esau's position in the family of Abraham was not lost, but his inheritance was lost. There was 'no place for repentance'. Once Jacob had taken the oath there was no possibility of a change of mind. Even weeping would not bring Esau back to precisely where he was before. Forgiveness was available. Eventually he wanted his inheritance but he left it too late. An oath had been taken. Repentance can bring forgiveness, but if God should ever 'swear in his wrath' (Hebrews 3:11), even repentance cannot bring back **opportunity**. Some will get to heaven 'saved through fire', safe themselves but with a story of lost opportunity.

However the writer of the letter to the Hebrews does not believe God has taken any 'oath of wrath'. They can still hear God's voice. So he moves on and in Hebrews 13 comes to practical details of the godly life they are to be led into. They must follow after holiness and pay attention to brotherly love, to hospitality, to honourable marriage, to freedom from love of money. The godly life is open to them. Let them heed the chastenings of God, and let God's strong and powerful hand lead them into their inheritance.

Chapter 18

Spiritual Warfare

Different people mean different things by the phrase 'spiritual warfare'. I personally like to keep as close as I can to Scripture so when I use the phrase I refer to Ephesians 6:10–20, which we look at in this chapter.

At the point in Ephesians where Paul brings in this call to spiritual battle he has already done two main things. He has put to the Ephesian Christians the 'exceeding greatness of God's power' which is at work in them (chapters 1–3) and he has appealed to them to work this out in the way in which they live (Ephesians 4:1–6:9). But he cannot stop there because there is a complicating factor. There is something – or someone – who makes this living of the Christian life difficult and Paul cannot close his letter until he has said something about it. So he adds 'Finally....' He has one last thing he must deal with. The Christian life ought to be simple. The power is given to us. We are taught how to live. There should be no problem. But *the devil is a complicating factor*. When we are saved we get a new Friend, but we also get a new enemy.

Look at Ephesians 6:10–11: '...Be strong in the Lord and in his mighty power. Put on the full armour of God....' There are three principles here.

1. **Fellowship**. We are told to be strong 'in' the Lord. This recalls what we have seen earlier (chapters 8, 9 and 12). We are 'in Christ'. Everything that has happened to him has happened to us. Now we are able to consciously

113

enjoy our fellowship with him. The secret of spiritual warfare begins with fellowship! It is no good our trying to
practise the instructions of verses 14–20 unless we enjoy our
position 'in Christ'.

2. **Trust**. We are to be strong in the Lord 'and in His
mighty power'. This means that as we enjoy our being
united to Jesus, and as we enjoy a fellowship with him that
may have its ups and downs but basically cannot be shat-
tered or altered, we are conscious that his mighty power is
at work on our behalf. Ours is the activity; ours is the
conflict. But his is the power. We are weak in ourselves but
we have strength in him. We move forward trusting that he
will provide the power.

3. It is only after Paul has said these two things that he
moves on to the third: **warfare**. He tells us to 'Put on the
whole armour....' This is a picture of warfare, of fighting.

He reminds us of the greatness of the battle. 'For our
struggle is not against flesh and blood, but against the
rulers, against the powers, against the world forces of this
darkness, against the spiritual forces of wickedness in the
heavenly places.' One of the great characteristics of the
devil is **cleverness**. He is like a snake that is difficult to see.
He is clever in hiding himself, and in using our weak points.

He attacks us at many points. He attacks the Church by
(a) neglect of Scripture, (b) deadness, (c) persecution,
(d) division.

He attacks the individual: in the body, in the mind (intel-
lectualism, error), in our experience (attacking assurance,
promoting false experiences), in our conduct (mistaken
directions, mistaken decisions, legalism, thoughtlessness).

It is the devil who is our ultimate enemy. We have three
enemies: the flesh, the world, the devil. The greatest is the
devil: '...our struggle is not against flesh and blood'. He
also has many assistants. '...rulers ... powers ... world
forces ... spiritual forces of wickedness....' There is a
variation in the devil's attacks. Sometimes the devil gives us
an easy time for a while. The battle is not always on one
level; but then he returns and we experience 'the evil day'.

Paul assures us that we can have victory, and are 'able to stand firm against the schemes of the devil,' 'able to resist in the evil day, and having done everything, to stand firm.' There is a battle. It may be hard sometimes, but we are able to win! The devil is resistable!

It is against this background that Paul calls us to spiritual warfare. There is a way of preparing for attack, and of standing under attack. We are to 'take up the full armour of God,' that we 'may be able to resist in the evil day.' The secret of victory is watchfulness and thoroughness: it is when we have 'done everything', we shall 'stand firm'.

Paul mentions the weapons we are to use. Five of them are defensive (belt, breastplate, shoes, shield, helmet), one of them is offensive (sword). Three of them you wear (belt, breastplate, shoes); three of them you 'take up' (shield, helmet, sword). Prayer is also mentioned, but it is not mentioned as a piece of armour. Paul did **not** say (for example): 'Use the spear of prayer.' Let us look at these six items.

1. **The belt of the truth.** This is not the same as the sword of the Spirit that comes later. In the ancient world people often wore long flapping robes. If they had to do anything energetic it was necessary to 'belt themselves together', to 'gird up their loins' (to use Bible language). In the Christian battle there is something that girds us, that holds us together, that prepares us for conflict. It is 'the truth', the 'whole counsel of God', the entire teaching of the gospel.

The 'sword of the Spirit' is a matter of using particular words from God, but the 'belt of truth' is the entire gospel.

We are vulnerable to the devil if we have not got a good grasp of the entire Christian faith in all of its length and breadth. We need to get to grips with God's Word. We need to read it systematically. We need to read it searchingly and questioningly. What did it mean when it was written? What is the teaching? What is the example I should follow or avoid? What does it mean to me now? Then we need to keep this belt on and constantly remind ourselves of the things we know.

2. **The breastplate of righteousness.** If the belt was something that held the entire body together, the breastplate was a piece of metal that covered the chest and the heart. In the ancient world it was the area that was associated with the feelings and the emotions.

The devil loves to attack our emotions and feelings. Perhaps his greatest weapon is discouragement.

Now the gospel of Jesus provides something that covers and protects us at this very point: we are righteous in Christ. The devil may attack our feelings, our emotions, our sense of assurance and peace, our confidence in the midst of battle. He likes to spread doubt and fear. But in the middle of the battle for holiness we remember that we are covered with the righteousness of Christ.

If I am covered with the righteousness of Christ then it means that my acceptance with God does not depend on how well I am doing; it depends on how well Jesus did.

If I am covered with the righteousness of Christ then it means that the ups and downs of my living a godly life, my successes and my failures, do not really affect my relationship with him. I need not feel that I have ruined everything if I find weakness in myself. I can get up if I fall. I am covered in all situations with the breastplate of Christ's righteousness.

3. **The shoes of peace.** If the belt holds me altogether, if the breastplate covers my heart, the shoes protect my feet and give me agility and speed. What are the shoes? They are the 'readiness' or the 'preparedness' of the gospel of peace. This seems to mean that I know I am at peace with God myself and I am ready to take it anywhere or speak it anywhere.

There is no one more able to get victory in the battle against the devil than one who has peace in his heart and who is eager and ready to share it and take it anywhere. The Romans invented sandals. Roman soldiers needed to be able to move fast to any corner of their empire to put down any rebellion. So they invented roads to walk on and sandals to use when walking on them. As a result they were the best soldiers of their day, irresistible, scarcely ever losing a battle.

We shall be like this if we have peace with God. What is peace? It is a sense of being right with God, an assurance of forgiveness. If we go out into battle ready with this testimony and this message, we are already in victory against Satan.

4. **The shield of faith.** We have seen three things that have to be permanently fixed on (belt, breastplate, shoes). Now we come to things that have to be 'taken up' in any time of particular attack or conflict.

What is the shield of faith? Has faith not already been implied in what Paul has said? The 'belt of truth' involves faith in Jesus. The 'breastplate of righteousness' is worn by faith in Jesus and his blood. What is meant is surely applying your faith to particular problems. When you are facing some particular temptation, to anxiety, to impurity, to greed, hold up the shield of faith! Ask yourself: what is that I believe in? What am I trusting for Jesus to do for me in this particular attack of the devil?

5. **The helmet of salvation.** The officers of the Roman army were famous for their plumed helmets. They could be seen miles away because of their bright colours. The helmet was the thing that made the Roman officer hold his head up high. He was a Roman! He was invincible! His armies had conquered the Mediterranean world. He knew that he was going to win!

There is an equivalent of all this in the life of the Christian. It is the expectation you have that you will win and get to glory. You are on the winning side. Jesus is with you. You have the best general in the world. You are part of an army that cannot fail. The helmet is the **expectation** of final salvation (1 Thessalonians 5:8 has the phrase 'the expectation of salvation').

6. **The sword of the Spirit.** This is not so much the Word of God as whole, as particular parts of the Word of God that relate to any crisis we are in. To use the sword of the Spirit is using particular scriptures against Satan, as Jesus

did when he was tempted. Jesus is the great example of how to use this aspect of the total armour of God. When attacked by the devil he drew on his knowledge of Scripture and applied particular verses to the conflict that he was going through.

When we are being tempted it is difficult to keep a clear mind. All sorts of justifications and rationalisations for sin come to us. But if we are in a habit of simply standing on what God has said we shall find that one text will hold us where a thousand arguments would let us down.

Jesus did not hold conversations with the devil or enter into debate with him. He simply took his stand on simple words that God had spoken. Man lives by every decision that proceeds from God; you shall not test the Lord; you shall worship the Lord (Matthew 4:4, 7, 10).

7. **Prayer.** This is not mentioned as **one** weapon, because it is going on all the time. Prayer has to be going on throughout the Christian's life, at many points of the day. It has to be 'in the Spirit', led by the Spirit, following the impulse of the Spirit, looking for the Spirit's empowering and guiding. Two subjects for prayer are specially mentioned: the need that we cover our fellow Christians ('for all the saints') and the need that we protect in prayer the preaching of God's Word ('and also for me, that utterance may be given me').

Chapter 19

Working Out the Details

'Working out the details' comes last for good reasons. All too often holiness is taught as a kind of dull moralism, a string of detailed rules and instructions. But the Bible does not do things this way. Take the letter to the Romans. There is not a single command in the book for the first five chapters or so; only in Romans 6:11. The commands do not really get going until chapter 12, and then the whole chapter is all words of exhortation.

In Paul's letters the detailed instructions tend to come at the end of the book. There is a reason for this. Our problem is not knowledge; it is power. It is not detailed information we need at first, it is knowledge of how we can live a godly life. It is to glimpse the 'mercies of God'. Only then will we be ready for the detailed instructions.

But we do get to the details eventually. The New Testament letters give a vast quantity of detailed advice and instruction on all sorts of spiritual matters, all of them practical and down-to-earth.

Think of it as we find it in the letter to the Ephesians. Paul introduces himself (1:1–2), then bursts into praise (1:3–14), sweepingly surveying the blessings of salvation. In Ephesians 1:15 he begins to write out a prayer that he is praying for the Ephesian Christians. It is a prayer that has long digressions in it and does not really end till the end of chapter 3. He prays for three things: (i) the certainty of their expectation of glory (1:18), (ii) the riches of their inheritance (1:18), and (iii) the surpassing greatness of God's power which is already at work in them (1:19a); the greatness of God's power which is at work in us who believe. This leads Paul to launch out on a massive exposition of the power of God. It is power seen in Jesus (1:19b–23); it is power seen in the new birth of Christians (2:1–10); it is power seen in the creation of the Church, despite all the barriers between Jews and gentiles (2:11–22). Then Paul starts up with his prayer again but has scarcely said a few words (3:1) before he digresses again! This time he wants to explain his call to the Christian preaching ministry and his relationship to the Christians at Ephesus (3:2–13). In Ephesians 3:14, he comes back to his prayer, finishes it, and ends with a doxology to God (3:14–21).

Notice that in all of this there has not been any very definite call to a life of godliness. Paul is more concerned that they should **first** know about the exceeding greatness of God's power at work in them. Only when they are quite clear about what has happened to them will he begin to call them to the godly life. In Ephesians 4:1 he is about half way through and starts now to call them to live a godly life. The thing he puts first is that they attend to securing harmony within the Church. There is to be harmony (4:1–3) with unity (4:4–6). He goes on to talk about the ministry-gifts within the Church and how it should lead to Christian maturity. If they attend to the teaching ministries they will be progressing towards the 'unity of the faith and of the knowledge of the Son of God'; they will be growing into the 'measure of the stature of the fullness of Christ' (4:7–16).

But he still has not fully put to them the basis for their hope of a godly life. He comes to it in Ephesians 4:17–24. They must be unlike the gentiles (4:17–19). Then he begins to explain the basis of their hope of godliness. They have 'learned Christ' (4:20). Translations of Ephesians 4:22–24 vary. They can be translated as commands (as in the Revised Standard Version) but I prefer to translate them as facts (in line with Romans 6):[1] 'so that you have put off the old man ... and are being renewed ... and you have put on

the new man . . . . ' The teaching is the same as that which
we have seen before in Romans chapter 6. The 'old person'
– the persons they used to be – have ceased altogether.
They are new people. They are being renewed. They are
risen with Christ. This is the secret of holiness. They are not
the people they used to be. They are in an entirely different
situation. They are not ruled by sin or Satan or law or death
or judgement. They are alive in Christ!

Now they are ready for the details! The sequence of
teaching is so vital. If you press godliness on people – or
upon yourself – without the teaching of Ephesians 1:1–4:25,
you are teaching a barren and fruitless moralism! In such a
case, there is no difference between your teaching and that
of the average members of the religions of the world. They
all teach morality – of varying sorts. Politicians are eager to
press 'good living' on the peoples of the world. Is the
Christian gospel no different? What makes the difference is
that the details of godliness are at the end and not at the
beginning! Pagan moralists **begin** with urging discipline and
morality and the rest. Secular minded politicians are only
too eager to press morality upon the people. Who wants to
rule a nation of criminals? But the distinctive mark of the
Christian gospel is that it talks about being risen with Christ
long before it gets down to the details of conduct. Paul gets
there eventually and so should we! Godliness does not take
care of itself – as many of us have learnt the hard way! But
we need to know our position before we start worrying
about details. We need the joy unspeakable and full of
glory that makes it somewhat easier to live the godly life.
Only then will Jesus' burden be easy and his yoke will be
light.

See how Paul now gets down to details. The plan of his
letter from this point can be set out as follows. He comes to
put forward six areas where there should be a great contrast
between what the Christian was and what he is now that he
knows Jesus. Paul has things to say about truth (Ephesians
4:25), about anger (4:26–27), about stealing and willingness
to work (4:28), about our talk (4:29–30), about kindness

(4:31–5:1) and about compromise with common sins (5:2–7).

Then he comes at it another way. The Christian is to be light in the world (5:8–17). Then there is yet another way of putting it; he is to be filled with the Holy Spirit (5:18–21).

Now he is ready to get down to some more practical details. Godly living involves following the leading of the Spirit in the most sensitive area of all: relationships with other people. So he goes into details with regard to the three most crucial sets of relationship: husbands and wives (5:22–33), children and parents (6:1–4), employers and employees in the most tricky kind of employment that there ever was – slavery (6:5–9)!

It is not my purpose to write a detailed exposition of all of this. My only point is: the New Testament has a mass of detail for us to work at. The Christian needs to 'work out his own salvation' in these many areas of life. This is what the New Testament was written for. It gives us a mass of detailed teaching about all manner of subjects. We have glanced at Ephesians only. It is not a law-book or an ethical manual. But it is putting into words what the leading of the Spirit will be in practice. The whole Bible has details about the godly life. We could consider Romans with its teaching about the state (13:1–7), or 1 Corinthians with its teaching about weakness of conscience and compromise with idolatry (1 Corinthians 8–10) and life in the Church (1 Corinthians 12–14). We could look at Paul's wonderful and staggering call to Christian love (1 Corinthians 13). We could spend many hours pondering the searching lines of the Sermon on the Mount, in Matthew chapters 5–7. Every part of the Bible gets down to practical details. The whole Bible is a manual of holiness. The whole Christian Church is a 'holiness movement'!

Endnotes

(1) For the scholarly details, see J. Murray, *Principles of Conduct*, 1957, pp. 214–219.

Chapter 20

'When All Around My Soul Gives Way...'

We all know what it is to fail. We may not have robbed a bank or run away with another man's wife – but we know what it is to fall far short of what we want to be in Jesus. If my salvation depended on how holy I felt I would not find much to give me assurance of salvation. Thank God assurance is in Jesus.

Perhaps you are conscious of your great failure. 'Why did I fail?' you ask.

(1) **Perhaps you do not realise that you will never be free of your need of the blood of Jesus Christ.**

How holy do you expect to be? Well, I can tell you one thing. You will never be so holy, in this life, that you do not need the blood of Jesus. 'I am writing' – said the apostle John – 'so that you may not sin.' But he immediately adds, 'but if anyone sins....' The Greek word 'if' when used with what the scholars call a subjunctive is often used to denote what is expected to occur! John does not want you to sin, but he immediately makes it clear that he knows you will. There is such a thing as maturity, there is all-round integrity of character. But the godliest of people never feel that they have arrived. John Wesley, a godly man, believed in a kind of 'perfection' of holiness but all of his life he never claimed it! 'If any man sins we have – already provided – an advocate with the Father, Jesus Christ the righteous and He is the propitiation for our sins.' You will need Jesus every day

123

of your life. You need him as your advocate. Don't try and dispense with him. Don't try to struggle to produce a day in your life when you say 'Today I did not sin. I don't need the blood of Jesus today!' Don't ever try to dispense with the blood of Jesus. You will need it every day of your life. The blood of Jesus is to be **used**. It is embarrassing day after day to need the blood of Jesus to cleanse us from sin. But don't get so 'holy' that you feel you don't need it. Accept that you are covered with the righteousness of Christ. Accept that you will be growing every day of your life. A friend of mine, many years ago, once asked me 'Pastor, is there any experience we can have such that we shall never sin again?' I replied 'Yes, there is. It is called **dying**.'

(2) **Perhaps you did not realise the depth of your own weakness**. It is true that in Christ you can do all things, but maybe it is taking you time to see that it is **in Christ** that you can do all things. In yourself, you are so, so, incredibly weak. You could be blown around like a light feather. You can be so mighty in Jesus and yet so weak in yourself. Learn to look to Jesus as your covering righteousness. Learn to look to Jesus for daily fellowship. Don't be a perfectionist. The very moment you forget that it is **in Christ** that you are strong, you will collapse. Fortunately he holds on to you. It is his job to hold on to you, as well as your job to hold on to him. Fortunately when we are faithless he is faithful. The most powerful resolutions will do you no good. If you were able to keep them it would only lead you into Pharisaism. Let your very failures teach you your own inherent weakness.

(3) **Perhaps you did not realise how much you needed fellowship with Jesus.** This is always where failure comes from. We are strong when we are rejoicing in Jesus, although even then temptations can rush round a corner with the violence of a hurricane.

> Temptations lose their power
> When Thou art nigh.
> I need Thee, O I need Thee!

Ev'ry hour I need Thee.
Oh, bless me now my Saviour!
I come to Thee.

It is true that you have 'died to sin' and are risen with Christ. But you still **need** fellowship with Jesus. Focus on him and everything will follow. He is your righteousness. He is your sanctification. Don't try to be holy outside of Jesus.

(4) **Perhaps you have not faced the fact that suffering is involved in breaking away from sin.** This is often where failure comes from. We are all addicts to selfishness and sinfulness. Admittedly some are more attracted to some sins than others. We can all think of sins we are not tempted to commit! But when it comes to the sins we have committed and that are so natural to us, it is going to involve suffering to break away. The way to break out of a bad habit is to face the fact that suffering is going to be involved.

(5) **Maybe your problem is that you have a divided will.** When all has been said and done I have to ask you: do you **want** to live a godly life? Could it be that your real trouble is that you want God to somehow force you. You are praying for victory over that one sin. You are saying that God is not answering your prayer. But the difficulty is perhaps that you don't want to get rid of it.

Face the truth! Are you really hungering and thirsting after righteousness? Don't whimper and say 'But I cannot deal with it.' Of course you can if you are 'in Christ'. Accept your position in Christ. Realise that you are seated in the heavenly places. Face the fact that it is dangerous to harden your heart, and to 'sin wilfully after coming to a knowledge of the truth.' Deal with that sin. Accept whatever suffering is involved. If you claim to be risen with Christ, then make a break now. Walk in newness of life.

(6) **Perhaps you need to realise what it means for God to work all things together for good.** Many years ago I made a big mistake. I was in a situation of great pressure. I asked

the Lord to do seven things for me, but I panicked and fled from that particular situation. Later on the Lord did all seven of the things I asked him to do, but I was no longer there to enjoy them! I learnt how serious it was to run away from a situation of trial, and how painful it is to miss something God wants to do through you.

Yet the strange thing is, God overruled it so marvellously. Everything about my present ministry which I enjoy so much I could not have got to – so it feels – without the mistake I made. I suppose Jonah could have said 'Those sailors would never have worshipped God if I had not been running away from him' (see Jonah 1:16).

But this is the amazing thing about God. He really does work everything together for good. Whatever your failure, whatever you have done, turn it utterly over to God. He may bring such good out of your past that it will seem that your past somehow had to be that way for you to get where God wants you to be.

There was a sick man once who was brought to Jesus by his friends (Matthew 9:1–8). The big thing the friends had on their minds was the sickness, but the thing that the sick man himself had on his mind was his sinfulness. When they all got to Jesus, Jesus said 'Son, be encouraged, your sins are forgiven.' He did at first not mention the sickness; he went to the man's real need – a fresh start in life by experiencing forgiveness. There was no word of rebuke. There was no talk about repentance. There were no conditions set, no time gap, no waiting. Immediately there was the slightest faith in the man's heart, Jesus said what needed to be said: 'Your sins are forgiven.'

The Pharisees were, of course, annoyed. They never do like grace. They did not like Jesus' friendliness to a sinner. They did not like the way in which Jesus seemed to imply it was **easy** to be forgiven. They did not like the immediacy and suddenness of the forgiveness. 'Let the man amend his life,' they would have liked to say. 'Let him prove that he has changed his ways! After a few months we might be able to accept him and – you never know – his physical state might improve a little! As for this Jesus, well it is easy to say that someone's sins are forgiven, but that is just words. We don't think anything has happened to the man at all!'

Jesus works the miracle of the healing. But it is worth noticing that:

(a) **the miracle illustrates the forgiveness!** They think Jesus has no authority. Well the miracle is worked 'so that you may know that the Son of Man has authority on earth to forgive sins.'

(b) **The miracle illustrates the power of forgiveness.** Here is a man broken with palsy, but also broken within by a sense of his own sinfulness. But the power that heals the body is the same power that can heal the guilt.

(c) **The miracle illustrates the speed of forgiveness.** How long does it take to work a miracle? How long does it take to forgive? In both cases – no time at all. You can be forgiven now – in the next few seconds.

(d) **The miracle illustrates the ease with which Jesus works.** How difficult is it for Jesus to work a miracle? How difficult is it for Jesus to forgive? Answer: in both cases, it is easy!

(e) **The miracle illustrates the grace and the generosity of Jesus.** How willing was Jesus to forgive? How willing was Jesus to heal? In both cases – Jesus' willingness was obvious. Without conditions, without ifs and buts, the man was liberated from his palsy, and liberated from his guilt.

(f) **The miracle illustrates the responsibility Jesus puts upon us.** When the man was healed, Jesus said to him, 'Now show that you have been healed. Take up your bed, and walk! Show that you are healed. Demonstrate your new ability. Walk around. Let everyone see.'

The same thing is true with regard to forgiveness. You may be forgiven now, you may be forgiven easily, you may be forgiven unconditionally, there need be no time gap. Believe now that Jesus is your advocate with the Father, that Jesus is the sacrifice that turns away all of God's displeasure over your sins. Believe it now!

But now also, get yourself on your feet and walk! Accept

total freedom from the guilt of your past sinful ways, and start walking in newness of life. And it will happen again, as it happened before. The multitudes will glorify God because of what they see in you.